STREAMING

STREAMING
An Education System in Miniature

BRIAN JACKSON

Volume 180

Routledge
Taylor & Francis Group

LONDON AND NEW YORK

First published in 1964

This edition first published in 2012
by Routledge
2 Park Square, Milton Park, Abingdon, Oxfordshire OX14 4RN

Simultaneously published in the USA and Canada
by Routledge
711 Third Avenue, New York, NY 10017

First issued in paperback 2014

Routledge is an imprint of the Taylor & Francis Group, an informa business

© 1964 Sonia Jackson

British Library Cataloguing in Publication Data
A catalogue record for this book is available from the British Library

ISBN 13: 978-0-415-50435-5 (Volume 180)
ISBN 13: 978-1-138-00826-7 (pbk)

Publisher's Note
The publisher has gone to great lengths to ensure the quality of this reprint but points out that some imperfections in the original copies may be apparent.

Disclaimer
The publisher has made every effort to trace copyright holders and would welcome correspondence from those they have been unable to trace.

STREAMING

*An Education System
in Miniature*

Brian Jackson

LONDON
ROUTLEDGE & KEGAN PAUL

First published 1964
by Routledge & Kegan Paul Limited
Broadway House, 68-74 Carter Lane
London, E.C.4

Printed in Great Britain
by W. & G. Baird Limited
London and Belfast

For
Christian and Lucy

CONTENTS

TABLES

Tables

ACKNOWLEDGEMENTS

THIS enquiry was made possible by a grant from the Joseph Rowntree Memorial Trust, and I am especially indebted to W. Wallace and L. Waddilove of that body.

I owe a great deal to the stimulus, even in conflict, I have had from Michael Young at the Institute of Community Studies, who was the first to urge me to pursue my ideas on selection by undertaking a small piece of research. And of the many people on whose help I have drawn, Jeremy Mulford, formerly Research Assistant at the Institute, put much bread-and-butter work into these enquiries and kindly tolerated my pursuit of many false trails.

Advice and help of many kinds has come from Gerry Anstock, Douglas Brown, Ann Cartwright, Peter Dean, Howard Dickinson, Muriel Donald, Elizabeth Grabham, Peter Marris, Dennis Marsden, Peter Willmott, Phyllis Willmott—and especially Peter Townsend. I have to thank the Institute's Advisory Committee, and the many children, parents, teachers and administrators who helped me in these enquiries.

In Cambridge my colleagues at the National Extension College and the Advisory Centre for Education never grudged me afternoons off, here and there, to write this book. As this was during difficult times when both ACE and the National Extension College were getting on their feet, it often meant that others took on more than their share of work. This was particularly true for Kathleen Hartley, Sonia Abrams and Ann Newton.

There is a special debt to W. B. Reddaway and the Department of Applied Economics at Cambridge. Without the quietness and space they have generously allowed me as visiting member there, I may have thought and talked a great deal about the selection of young children. But I certainly would not have been able to write.

BRIAN JACKSON

Advisory Centre for Education,
Cambridge,
August, 1964.

1

PROLOGUE: IN THE CLASSROOM

L ET me begin with a personal story. It may help to clarify the impulse from which this enquiry stemmed.

My first experience as a primary school teacher was a series of practice lessons in what had been my old 'council school'. I started with a much-prepared lesson on the mediaeval ballad, *Sir Patrick Spens*.

> The King sat in Dunfermline town
> Drinking the blood-red wine.
> O whare will I get a skeely skipper
> To sail this new ship o' mine.

The children mimed it as first myself—and then, after practice, a small girl with tight blonde pigtails—declaimed it. The teacher's chair became the royal throne of Scotland, desks were pushed back to reveal Leith sands, and blackboard and bookcase built the ship that had to sail the winter seas and fetch back the Princess of Norway.

> They hadna sail'd a league, a league,
> A league but barely three,
> When the sky grew dark and the wind blew loud,
> And gurly grew the sea.

Hunched groups moaned and whistled the storm from the classroom corners: a tallish boy stood by, switching the electric light on and off as if lightning flickered, almost dancing as he did so. And so the ship sank, the Scottish nobles drowned, and only their feather beds floated on the foam.

> And lang, lang may the maidens sit
> Wi' their gowd kames in their hair,
> A-waiting for their ain dear loves
> For them they'll see nae mair.

1

Crop-haired Yorkshire girls, swept imaginary combs through imaginary tresses . . .

It didn't last. The children tired and the lesson ended untidily. I was more excited than they were, looking forward to term after term keyed at this pitch. It had begun suspiciously easily. But I was far too pleased with myself to note that.

Twelve years before when I left this school myself there had been one class of fifty children for each year from seven to eleven; after that some passed their 'scholarship' to the grammar school and classes of thirty children for each year from twelve to fourteen were left behind. This was the old type of all-age school that has been gradually disappearing since the 1944 Education Act. That Act created the separate primary school for children from five to eleven. My old school turned into a primary, and its intake increased to fill the extra space. It now had three classes of children for each age group. Children were placed in their class according to ability, the idea being that the brightest children should be taught altogether in the 'A' class, the average ones in the 'B' class, and the weakest children in the 'C' class. They were 'streamed'.

This was the first time I encountered the streaming of young children, and far from being delighted or outraged, I must admit that I hardly noticed it. This is what I mean by saying there were questions I didn't ask. Those practice lessons that pleased me so much were all taken with 'A' stream classes. The boys and girls were eager, apt and docile: they presented few problems of order or apathy. Perhaps behind them were home backgrounds helpful to schooling, sanctions from parents and friends supporting their teacher, years of training at home and at school preparing them to attend to classroom work. Their habits, ambitions and needs intertwined and went along with what the teacher offered. A great deal of what I imagined I had done in taking *Sir Patrick Spens* with them—the creation and exploitation of an atmosphere of 'learning readiness'—was done, long before my arrival, by many people from fellow teachers to parents and even grandparents, and the schools, colleges and teachers that *they* had known long ago.

Glancing back at such lessons I wonder if they went quite as deep as I thought. Did the children accept, enjoy and dismiss them as 'holiday' periods remote from the important work of morning arithmetic and eleven plus intelligence tests? Were they perhaps more peripheral and decorative than I realised?

If I didn't learn from apparent success I should have done from apparent defeat. I didn't. Yet there was certainly one defeat in those first practice lessons. For a single period I was given what must have been the 'B' or 'C' stream—I imagine the 'C', but it is characteristic that I didn't know. With them I was taking a geography period on 'Rivers of Africa' and had begun by reading them Kipling's story of 'How the Elephant got its trunk' with its refrain of

the great, gray-green, greasy Limpopo river

and its tale of the Elephant Child who, in the days when elephants had no trunks, was scolded, pushed, bullied, and beaten by every animal in the jungle—and all for asking the harmless question 'What does the crocodile have for dinner?' My lesson was supposed to lead out from the refrain of the great Limpopo river. But I was as chagrined by its blank reception at each repetition, as I was taken aback at the shout of delight when I told how Elephant Child, with his tiny nose stretched out into the very first elephant trunk by a hungry crocodile, had returned to the jungle and spanked and bashed parents and relations, friends, enemies and neighbours. Instead of always being pushed around and pressed to the bottom, Elephant Child with his new trunk thrashed the whole adult world until it learned to treat him with a fresh respect.

That might have set me thinking about the natural 'subjection' of children, and the further subjection, necessary or unnecessary, involved in being a 'C' stream child. Perhaps it did, but at the time and for some while after, I gave over much more thought to the way this lesson crumbled into pieces. I put down Kipling, and drawing a map of Africa on the blackboard I began my set story-question-and-answer on African rivers . . . Limpopo, Niger, Congo, Nile.

I had completely lost my hold on that class before I became aware of it. After five or ten minutes I realised that I was the only one interested in African rivers. Not that boys were breaking windows or girls dancing on the top of desks: nothing like that. All the children were in their seats and looking at me, most of them were smiling but none of them was listening. I introduced the subject of the Niger as vividly as I could, but when I paused and asked questions, it was clear that no one had heard a word. A small boy with a pink eye-shield over his left eye sat in the front row, and as I moved on from Niger to Congo he grinned quite broadly and swaying his head almost rhythmically from side to side shot out grins to left and right that rippled back through his classmates. The tensions of the class circled round him—I don't know why—and they were ranged behind him, united as a group against the teacher. The lesson soon slipped past this point of amused uninterest: the smiles (except for the boy in the eye-shield) all faded, feet began to shuffle, unplaceable whispers flickered across the room. I began watching the clock. A worn tennis ball came slowly rolling down the middle aisle towards my feet. Should I demand to know from whom and where and why? I picked it up; then put it on the desk and returned to the Nile, the Blue Nile, the White Nile, the Mountains of the Moon. The class moved inevitably towards eruption; and then the lunchtime bell rang, slightly late. I rapidly dismissed them, and with a great clatter, boys and girls surged out, over desks and chairs, through the writhing squash at the door, through the corridor race, and with a final burst, out into the yard and the open air.

Immediately I was furious: angry that I hadn't called them back and had them file out properly. I don't suppose I'd ever seen a 'C' class burst out of school before, and I was baffled. Since then I've several times seen a 'C' class, when for some reason restraint has been lifted, thrust its way forward and almost explode into the playground whilst the 'A' class had gradually sauntered out behind it.

I consulted the 'C' stream teacher about my lesson. He thought it had been too fancy, not bread-and-butter enough. I should have made the children chant the names of the rivers after me, until more could repeat the list than couldn't. That would take most of the time, and then I might have filled up by telling them one thing about each river. And I should certainly have stopped the lesson, seized on a scapegoat, read the Riot Act, and inflicted as punishment four or five minutes total silence—and then back to the chant. He strongly advised me to learn the importance of simulating a towering rage: stamp,

4

bang, slam, shout. At the time I was impressed by much of his advice.

Fortunately I did not have to face another such challenge until I had been teaching for two years, and by then I had other reserves to call upon. My first full-time post was in a much smaller village school that had only one class to each year group: so of necessity the children were unstreamed. Whether I took arithmetic, history, religious instruction, or games the same children sat side by side in the same classroom. Of course they didn't do the same work or move at the same pace. To begin with I placed them in three or four groups for subjects such as reading and arithmetic: 'streaming' within the class, if you like. Ivan might be in the top group for arithmetic and the bottom group for reading, Christine was the other way round. But I must admit that most children tended to be in similar groups for all subjects: the home and personality that had helped or hindered them in reading, had also helped or hindered their mastery of numbers. Gradually, as skill and confidence developed, the groups dropped away and I found that 35 different children could each move at his own speed and still remain a class. If it had been a question of 45 or 55 this might never have happened.

Naturally there were behaviour problems. My first class contained one of the few very naughty girls I've met in school. She wasn't malicious but she was a considerable nuisance along traditional lines. The trouble was she had a fussily house-proud mother whose cramping demands for cleanliness, tidiness, neatness and propriety made home miserable for her. One morning after she'd crept in during playbreak and placed tin tacks on almost everyone's seat, I asked her 'Jenni, what's the most wicked thing you've ever done?' and she replied, 'The day I wasn't looking and spilled my raspberry jam on Mummy's best carpet.' There were also the more unsavoury thefts and meannesses of Gordon, but his was an equally pitiful situation. The local policeman was watching him, and Gordon knew he was watching him, because of his friendship with a convicted homosexual who lived alone on a nearby caravan site. And there was Roger too who mutinied, bullied, and destroyed, and who loved a knife in the way most boys love food. The point about these more difficult children, whether they were aggressive or recessive, was that their misdeeds were cushioned by the good behaviour and positive attitudes of the others. In that class I had time to see their troubles in perspective, to think of them in individual terms. I suppose that the presence of contented, busy children around them helped Jenni and Gordon and Roger to come to some terms with life. Yet what would a classful of Jennis and Gordons and Rogers be like, I wondered? Would they have helped each other?

But I can't say that I gave any thought during the next two years to 'streaming'. I was far to absorbed developing classroom methods, far too fascinated by individual relationships to stand back and survey classrooms from a distance. I was caught up by the great advance there'd been in teaching method since I was a boy. Even the three Rs—reading, writing and arithmetic—were quite different. I had myself been taught to read by phonetic methods—'b' as in bat, 'c' as in cat, 'd' as in dad, and no doubt there is still a place for such techniques. But it is common experience that a child of five or six can be taught to read quite long words—'elephant', 'aeroplane', 'blackboard', if they are meaningful to him, and especially if they have a *memorable shape*. Indeed there is a famous 'long word' in the opening of Beatrix Potter's *The Tale of the Flopsy Bunnies* that very tiny children learn to read, because it is highly memorable, and *looks* distinctive.

> 'It is said that the effect of eating too much lettuce is "soporific"...'

The method that is developed out of this way of learning to read is called 'look and say', and like every other teacher I had to work out that combination of phonetics and 'look and say' which best matched for my classes the irregular logic of the English language. And then there were skills to be developed concerning the measurement of 'reading ages', the detection of backward readers, and the discovery of ways to help them overcome weaknesses. This knowledge, and the ability to apply it, was extremely important and very rewarding, though not the slightest bit of use to me until the human relationship and the classroom atmosphere were right. Even so, I often couldn't get adequate reading books for boys such as Brian and Gordon (the 'C' children if you like). They needed books whose vocabulary was suited to a very beginner of five or six, and yet whose story would fully engage the attention of a lusty ten year old—books which were far more lavish and colourful than usual. There are very few such books on the market, and the ideal tools I required would certainly have been costly to produce. I sometimes grumbled that publishers who were drawing £10,000 a year from the sale of eleven plus crammers in English and arithmetic ought to be obliged to provide this basic equipment too.

Arithmetic was just as absorbing. It was astonishing to discover how the grading of the many different steps in a division sum could open up elementary mathematics to boys and girls who in my own school days would have been dismissed to deliver the milk crates and tidy the rabbit hutches with the obscure tag 'number blind'. Again it was a question of marrying the old and the new. The old held dominance in the classroom on my far right, where children chanted their tables from two-times-two to twelve-times-twelve, forwards and backwards, morning after morning. The children built their own primitive music out of it, but logic insisted that it was an unnecessarily complicated way of learning a limited number of facts. Through the partition to my left came the tap and clatter of coloured blocks, rods and beads where a younger class was learning arithmetic not by rote, but by *doing*. It was startling to see very tiny children approaching numbers in terms of concepts and relationships, and watch them successfully multiplying fractions by moving around bright, coloured strips of wood.

There was a great deal else to learn and master too, especially in the teaching of English, of physical exercise, of dance, drama and elementary science. It was evident that more could be done in the primary school than had been realised in previous years: my sense of the young child's potentiality was enormously enhanced—given the ideal environment, what *were* its limits? I'm not thinking in terms of what mountains of factual knowledge an apt and docile child can absorb, of how early it can start French, or use the semi-colon, or tackle simultaneous equations. Some, no doubt, will never do any of these things. But I'm thinking of the all-round development of the personality, not so

7

much of skill and pace as of the deeper quality of growth under-lying them—imagination and self-awareness. The right words are hard to find.

It is a mark of my inexperience that I was so fully absorbed in this work that I was barely conscious of the fact that what many teachers would have called 'work' was almost totally ab-sent from the school. What I seldom took into account was the fact that the school was in a country village and had so little success in the eleven plus examination that those papers were a very minor event indeed. It was far from the pressures of any rival school, ambitious parents sent their children elsewhere, the headmistress was moving towards retirement and she was long past the vanities of promotion and 'name'.

When the time came to move to a new school, I took a post in a large streamed establishment in the city. Platt Grove was usually big enough to have three classes to a year—'A' stream, 'B' stream, and 'C' stream. Whilst I was there, I spent only a minority of my time with 'A' children, most of it was with 'B's and 'C's. By now I had developed teaching resources which caught some of the interest and met some of the needs of the children placed in lower streams; and I found new fascination in offering fresh modes of teaching to classes which contained a good share of the rebellious, the apathetic and the weak. Let me take you around one such class of ten-year-old 'C' stream boys.

Here is Philip. He is small for his age, and came into the classroom crying this morning. A boy from the 'A' class, equally small, had been pushing him, not very hard. Philip has been filling in his diary: *'Last night I had my tea and watched TV and went to bed. The End.'* The spelling is correct because he has asked me for every second word. Above the writing is a feeble pencil drawing showing Philip (very large), his mother, father and brother (rather small) and their television set (very large). He has a reading age of six, but in recent weeks this has begun to rise. Pinned to the wall above him is a painting, two foot by three foot, of a rainbow over the ocean. A pencil is too fine an instrument for him to control, but given a large sheet of paper, a thick brush, vivid jars of colours and lots of elbow-room, he has painted a clumsy yet oddly beautiful picture. Underneath it I've stuck one of the little gold stars of merit with which I make rather free. Philip now and again glances up

8

at his painting and smiles at it quite openly. Yesterday he sneaked in at lunchtime 'to see the drawing pins hadn't fallen out of it'. Philip has a younger brother who is both cleverer and taller than he is. I have never seen their father or mother.

Behind Philip sits Jan. Jan's father is Polish, and Jan's English, though adventurous, is highly idiosyncratic. Jan has quarrels out of school with the other boys that I can never quite understand. In class he attracts a mild hostility broken by waves of elusive, guilty friendship. I notice this when he bruises his leg, badly too, against the ironwork of his worn, brown desk. Many of the other boys are quite pleased, and then—all in a rush—solicitous. On the other hand, Jan's slight isolation helps him to concentrate on his work. In his diary he embroiders genuine personal incidents:

> On Saturday I went to my friend and we go in Ross Street because I must clean car.
> When I and him finish we go back home. Nearly at the bridge I see three men drink whisky and therewas come policeman and one said look copper come, and another take a bottle and throw right on his head. Another push him and him fall over. Then those men start dancing round him. And one boy see that and go tell another police. When these men see police he run away.

His strong subject is arithmetic, at which he is rapid and intelligent. Unfortunately he often copies figures down from the blackboard carelessly, and more than once I've been irritated with him. Only recently I wondered about his eyesight. Now he wears glasses, and gets much of his arithmetic right. He may have been teased about the glasses, for he hates them and will push them under the desk lid if I'm not looking. He thinks I'm partly responsible for them, and dislikes me for it. Yet Jan has made much more progress this year than many of his classmates. His very loneliness liberates him from the low aspirations of many of the others.

By Jan sits Albert, another boy who dislikes me, as he does all the rest of officialdom. I have never handled Albert well, and in the business of other children's dilemmas I have never found the time to think his situation through. Albert is a well-built boy, quite assertive amongst his own group of friends. Yet curiously enough he always refers to the 'A' class as 'the big boys': he likes taking messages to their classroom, though I don't think he has any friends there. There's often the smell of urine around Albert, and I send him home with wet pants several times a term. From his diary I discover that he is learning to play percussion in the Salvation Army band. His parents never come near the school. The headmaster believes that his father is blind, and that his mother earns the wage. But we don't know.

I am scrupulous about dividing my time fairly between the boys, and about showing the same face to all of them; but in my heart of hearts I know that I turn from Albert to Martin with some relief. I am conscious of having had more success with Martin than with anyone else in the class. After only a few weeks' teaching I knew that Martin was rising out of that resistant mesh of minimum standards. Perhaps something had suddenly clicked into place in Martin's life, far away from lessons and classrooms. His arithmetic which had been years behind is very rapidly improving: in six months he might come close to an average standard. Yet it isn't his arithmetic that excites me. I often look at the very lovely painting of a still, fenland pool that is pinned above his desk. There is shadowed water, edged by rushes and overarched by trees, and across one side of the pool he has scrawled his own account in words.

> The sky was thrush egg blue with a few mistletoe white clouds scudding across the burning sun. The sunlight glistened down through the spring leaves and reflected on the silver surface of the pool.
> A thundering waterfall could be heard in the distance but here a few fish were quietly waving their silky fins. A gold dragonfly hovered nearby and a fat round toad flopped into the water from a millstone. There were pink blossoms and one or two leaves floating there.

Every word is as he wrote it on the painting, and with none of them did I give him any help. Evidently the creative impulse wasn't there when he first joined the 'C' class. It rarely shows itself like this. Very shortly Martin will go to the secondary modern school. Once there, will he retreat into his 'C' stream shell or not? I don't know. The headmaster thinks it would be unwise to uproot him into the 'B' stream at this late stage, and I agree. But if there was this in Martin, we wonder sometimes which other children here contain untapped reserves of life.

I had not, for instance, suspected that Kevin was a child of any ability. But near the beginning of the year I gave the children a non-verbal intelligence test. It was one of Raven's Matrices in which the boys had to pick out missing parts from different, coloured patterns. According to his score, Kevin was placed in the top five per cent. of any random selection of children. Yet here he was lost somewhere in the bottom ten per cent. I was quite unable to understand this, for in every way he struck me as a poorly-endowed child. Yet, more slowly and less masterfully than Martin (who did badly on that test), he too has begun to write with some confidence:

As I walked home I had to cross the field. And as it came into the sparkling moonlight the dew shone. It looked like wavering golden and silver slopes. I crossed over the field. I was nearly home and I could see the windows of my home likely golden glas. I could see all the big wall glitring in the moonlight. I got close to my home, touched the golden doorhandle, twisted it round and went in.

Kevin's spiky handwriting is very untidy. The pen is not under his control. He holds it awkwardly, so tightly, that his finger joints are tense and white. I allow him the luxury of pencil. Kevin had a mild attack of polio when he was five or six. His mother is a widow.

There is also Barry: in nine months I feel I've taught him very little. He is absent about one day a fortnight, which is encouraging for the figure had been one day in three for several years. He is very susceptible to the leadership of other boys, and some of my most difficult pupils have had a poor effect on him. No one has ever seen his mother, and his father has never returned to the school since he first enrolled Barry. He is remembered because when we asked him the child's age and birthday, he turned angrily on the boy and shouted 'How old are you? When's your birthday?', and neither of them knew. Barry has five brothers and two sisters.

To the visitor's eye the class looks a busy set of children, throwing up modest achievements by the way. Certainly pains have been taken to display Philip's painting, Henry's handwriting, Jan's mosaic, Gerald's nature notes . . . Yet there is pitifully little to take pleasure in here. There is too much hindered or stunted growth in the room. Sometimes I think that this is simply the human condition, and there is no more to be said.

But I also begin to wonder whether it is a good thing to group these children together as a 'C' class. Does it help me to concentrate on their problems, and to set a better pace? Or does it increase those problems, firstly for the children, by imposing a third-class position on to them and secondly for the teacher by facing him with an interlocking net of handicaps? Would they find it easier to grow and establish relationships if they worked amongst a class community of more stable, and often more gifted people than themselves? Or would work alongside such children only breed anxiety and despair? And what do the more fortunate children lose or gain by being penned in their 'A' stream? Are their academic standards higher? Are their values any different?

As these questions emerge, certain points have already become clear. Firstly, the class of boys such as I have just described, had been streamed at 7 years of age with considerable care and experience. It was a thoughtful process, based on tests and reports, and neither headteacher nor class teacher spared their energies in drawing up the final lists. Secondly, I nevertheless came to know that this particular 'C' class contained some extremely gifted children; and I have re-discovered this, after a time, with other 'B' or 'C' classes. Thirdly, though there were some successes with such children, the achievements were in the end very limited ones. For though you could at times create an atmosphere in which Albert and Jan and Kevin and Philip believed they had quite as much dignity as 'A' children, and sometimes perhaps, talents of their own, yet outside the classroom this self-confidence soon disappeared.

Two years later I took leave of absence from my school in order to explore problems arising out of my own background and education. During the course of writing the book which emerged from those interests, I found myself visiting other primary schools and considering streaming from a distance. Released from the rush of classroom work I sometimes saw patterns that I would never have noticed as a class teacher. 'C' class after 'C' class was so similar, 'A' class after 'A' class was so alike, that I wondered if there was more to streaming than a device for grouping apart the academically strong and the academically weak. Quite what kind of a social mechanism was it? Quite what kind of boy or girl fared well or badly under it?

I felt that if there was one piece of educational research that ought to be undertaken for the primary school it was an enquiry into streaming. Fortunately others felt the same and in the last few years we've learned a lot about streaming. The following contribution—a series of linked essays—aims to produce a few more facts. But its chief concern is to look at the values that create streaming and to consider some of the possible losses and gains that lie beyond statistical reach. Even if streaming as we know it came to an end, it seems likely that this mesh of values would continually produce other systems and devices with the same effects. Streaming is our education system in miniature.

2

660 SCHOOLS

How widespread is streaming today? How does it work and how is it justified? I wondered how typical my own teaching experiences had been. A teacher's vision of his children may be penetrating in depth. He may know a great deal about them as individuals: which girl has to be brought to the school gates by her mother, which boy spends all his leisure in the lonely pleasures of cycling, who collects cigarette cards, and who is heading for the juvenile court. But there are things he cannot easily see. It is difficult to know children over their life-span. He teaches them as a class of eleven year olds: but he cannot usually follow them on to 12, 13, 14, 15, 16, 17, 18 and adult life. To some extent his own contribution is invested, hopefully, in the dark, not knowing what kind of men and women he is helping to nourish. The forefront is continually filled by new classes of boys and girls, and the old dissolve away.

It seemed that the next thing to do was to discover a little about the national situation and see if there were any factors at work not easily observed in the classroom.

In 1962 4,129,578 children attended 23,191 different primary schools in England and Wales. Many of these schools were too small to stream, even if they wished to. It seems reasonable to say that most primary schools with 300 children aged between 7 and 11 face the choice of streaming or not streaming the whole school. Most schools below this size either cannot stream, or can only partially stream. There were 2,892 schools which, so far as one could see, probably had the opportunity to fully stream. With the aid of the Ministry we drew a sample of one in three, and despatched a questionnaire to 964 schools in 126 different education authorities. Six hundred and sixty schools from 108 different authorities returned a completed questionnaire. Between them they contain about a quarter of a million pupils.

I do not know how representative these schools are. Several authorities, of which the most important were Bristol, Sheffield, Middlesex, Manchester, Sussex, Liverpool and Northumberland did not co-operate. This accounts for the failure of 144 schools to respond. An important weakness is that these areas could differ considerably from the country as a whole—For example they might contain larger proportion of unstreamed schools. I do not think this is so, but the caution needs remembering. A further 160 schools refused or did not reply.[1] Again I not know for certain why this was. Partly it was because I was not permitted to send them reminder notices. Sometimes schools wrote back to say the head was ill, the buildings were being altered and so on. But I believe that much resistance was aroused by questions on Fathers' occupation. Some Heads denounced this part of the enquiry in their local press, and many were disinclined to complete a questionnaire which not only required quite a lot of work, but sometimes asked for information which they did not possess and which they did not like to seek.

The sample discussed in this and the next chapter reports the picture as it was in 1962. It is national and largely urban[2] It has considerable weaknesses. These must not be overlooked, and I state them now so that I do not have to append them to every future statement.

How many primary schools streamed children?

One third of the questionnaires were sent to head teachers; one third went to 'A' stream teachers and one third to the teacher of the lowest stream. If the school were not streamed the head was asked to give the questionnaire to any class teacher. There was no difference in the refusal rate between the different groups. The schools were first asked whether they streamed or did not stream their children.

[1] Unfortunately the Ministry was not prepared to give me addresses of schools, only their official code number. I then had to ask each authority if they would forward the questionnaires to the schools whose code number I possessed. This meant that at this stage of the enquiry I had no direct contact with the schools, and could not for example discover why questionnaires had not been completed. It was only very much later in the enquiries the authorities allowed me the names and addresses I requested.

[2] 82 per cent. of all primary school children live in urban areas.

TABLE 1

ENGLAND AND WALES: PERCENTAGE OF STREAMED AND
UNSTREAMED SCHOOLS IN A SAMPLE OF 660

Streamed schools	96%
Unstreamed schools	4%
Total %	100

The overwhelming majority of these schools chose to stream. But at what age?

TABLE 2

AGE AT WHICH CHILDREN WERE STREAMED

Already streamed on arrival from:	
Infants' department	50%
streamed by seven years	74%
streamed by eight years	87%
streamed by nine years	92%
streamed by ten years	96%
Number of schools	633

Half the children had already been graded before they arrived in the junior school. Almost three quarters were streamed by about the age of seven. By the final year it was almost universal.

If so many children were graded when they left the infant school, how many were actually graded *in* that school before the age of seven? The sample did not include any separate infant schools, but it did contain 134 combined infant and junior schools and in these even earlier streaming did take place.

TABLE 3

STREAMING OF INFANTS IN JUNIOR WITH INFANT SCHOOLS

Streamed at five years	5%
Streamed at six years	25%
Number of schools	134

In establishing the extent and age of streaming, there is a danger that what is charted was obvious to start with and required no painstaking research. As a check on this 38 teachers who were attending a course which dealt with streaming were told of the sample, given the above tables without the numbers, and asked to fill in the percentages experience had taught them to expect. This was a special and highly informed sample of teachers whom we would expect to get nearer the truth than the average class teacher.

TABLE 4

	Experienced Teachers' Estimates			Sample Figure
Age by which pupils were streamed	Average	Minimum	Maximum	
7 years	48%	0%	100%	74%
8 years	62%	3%	100%	87%
9 years	73%	15%	100%	92%
10 years	78%	15%	100%	95%

On the whole these experienced teachers underestimated the amount of streaming by about 20 per cent. Moreover the *spread* of estimates was extremely wide, and whereas some believed that *no* seven year old children were streamed, others estimated that *all* these seven year olds were. The degree to which streaming has penetrated the educational system may not have been realised, even by the very experienced, and the individual teacher may be limited by his experience more than he realises.[1]

How are streams decided?

How are these children classified as 'A', 'B' and 'C'? A pilot enquiry[2] suggested that ten different methods were being used in a variety of combinations. These included:

[1] A further sample test of 81 teachers in training conducted by my colleague Jeremy Mulford, showed an 'error' of 40-50 per cent., compared to the 'error' of about 20 per cent. made here by very experienced teachers.

[2] Jackson, B., 'Teachers' Views on Primary School Streaming', *Educational Research*, November, 1961.

1. An Infant School Report
2. A class teacher's recommendation
3. The 'experienced judgment' of a head teacher and staff.

These three directly involved the teacher's personal assessment of the child; but I know little of what they amounted to in detail.

4. A school arithmetic test
5. A school reading test
6. A school English test.

Again it was impossible to know what this might mean in practice. One school arithmetic test might be based on pounds, shillings and pence sums, another on 'tables', another on simple problems, and the standard could vary vastly from place to place.

Finally there were four common kinds of external measurements:

7. An external intelligence test
8. An external reading test
9. An external arithmetic test
10. An external spelling test.

These tests were named by the schools (Moray House Picture Test, Schonell Graded Word Reading Test, and so on) and having been properly prepared and standardised over a wide range of children, would give results of a more objective kind.

Table 5 shows the popularity of the ten methods:

TABLE 5
PERCENTAGE OF SCHOOLS USING EACH METHOD

1. Class Teacher's Recommendation	79%
2. Infant School Report	67%
3. School Arithmetic Test	57%
4. School English Test	56%
5. 'Experienced Judgment'	55%
6. External Reading Test	54%
7. External Intelligence Test	43%
8. School Reading Test	42%
9. External Arithmetic Test	28%
10. External Spelling Test	21%

Number of schools supplying this information   593

A large number of schools preferred to group children as 'A', 'B' or 'C' without much use of objective tests: 37 per cent. used none at all. The most popular methods were all 'internal': private to the school concerned. Less than half the schools employed an intelligence test.

School class and social class

Having examined the extent of the streaming principle, and the variety of methods that lead up to an 'A', 'B' or 'C' grading, we can stand back a little and look for other factors at work. If the individual class teacher were asked about the 'A', 'B', 'C' divisions, he might reply that the very able children were placed in the 'A' stream, the average ones in the 'B' stream, and the below average ones in the 'C' stream. But can we isolate other things that these children have in common so as to illuminate what 'very able', or 'B' or 'below average' mean?

One obvious factor is social class. The teachers were therefore asked for to give the fathers' occupation. Heads supplied this information for all their first year classes, teachers for the one final year class of which they were in charge. I think this request was the main single reason why some schools did not

TABLE 6

11 YEAR OLD CHILDREN: FATHERS' OCCUPATION IN 140 TWO-STREAM SCHOOLS

Fathers' Occupation	*'A' stream*	*'B' stream*	*Total* %
Professional and Managerial	73%	27%	100%
Clerical	61%	39%	100%
Skilled Manual	56%	44%	100%
Semi-skilled Manual	42%	58%	100%
Unskilled Manual	39%	61%	100%
Percentage of children in each stream	53%	47%	100%
Total number of 11 year old children sampled	5,285		

answer the questionnaire. Obviously the answers received must contain some element of bias or misreporting. They were difficult to check, but spot tests suggested that the returns were fairly accurate so far as professional, managerial and unskilled workers were concerned. But I suspect an element of skilled workers had not had their jobs recorded properly and have been included in the semi-skilled category.

Remembering this weakness, the returns from 140 two-stream schools are set out in Table 6 above.

Streaming placed the middle-class child[1] in the 'A' rather than the 'B' stream, and this was also true (though only just) of the skilled manual group.

The same pattern was found in the three-stream school:

TABLE 7

11 YEAR OLD CHILDREN: FATHERS' OCCUPATION IN 252
THREE-STREAM SCHOOLS

Fathers' Occupation	'A' stream	'B' stream	'C' stream	Total %
Professional and Managerial	58%	28%	14%	100%
Clerical	47%	32%	21%	100%
Skilled Manual	41%	35%	24%	100%
Semi-skilled Manual	29%	41%	30%	100%
Unskilled Manual	21%	34%	46%	100%
Percentage of children in each stream	37%	36%	27%	100%
Total number of 11 year old children sampled	14,200			

In Table 7, the chances of Professional parents' children entering the lowest of three streams are only 14 in a 100; and again the skilled manual group is slightly on the more favoured

1 In this discussion, non-manual workers are called 'middle class' and manual workers 'working class'. This is, of course, an arbitrary measure, but it is not easy to define a more delicate one without becoming more complex than the evidence here merits.

side, leaving the largest percentage of the children of semi-skilled fathers in the 'B' class and of unskilled fathers in the 'C'.

The four stream school displays the same trend; every extension of streaming increasing the above-average chances of the young middle-class pupil:

TABLE 8

11 YEAR OLD CHILDREN: FATHERS' OCCUPATION IN 228 FOUR-STREAM SCHOOLS

Fathers' Occupation	'A' stream	'B' stream	'C' stream	'D' stream	Total %
Professional and Managerial	55%	17%	13%	5%	100%
Clerical	40%	32%	17%	11%	100%
Skilled Manual	34%	30%	24%	12%	100%
Semi-skilled Manual	20%	28%	31%	21%	100%
Unskilled Manual	14%	24%	30%	32%	100%
Percentage of children in each stream	30%	28%	25%	17%	100%
Total number of children sampled			7,097		

In the four-stream school, the professional or manager's child has 95 chances in a 100 of not being in the 'D' stream, whereas a third of the labourer's children end up there, even though the numbers in this school class are relatively small. Once a mixed ability group is divided into an 'A' and 'B' stream, the professional man's child takes 20 per cent. more than his numerical 'share' of 'A' stream places. If they are divided into 'A', 'B', 'C' and 'D' groups, he claims 25 per cent. more. And once more the rough-and-ready 'class' line between clerical and skilled manual is blurred a little, leaving the semi-skilled and unskilled as a distinct group whose children move

21

chiefly into the lower streams. These analyses illustrate the considerable reinforcement of social differences created by primary school streaming.[1]

Further analyses of 24 schools which had five, six, or seven streams confirmed these trends. The 'G' stream child was almost always from the humbler working-class home.

Not all children had fathers, or had fathers with jobs. Here my information was very scanty. There were children whose mothers were widows or whose fathers were unemployed, missing, in prison or mentally ill. The proportion in the various streams was as follows:

TABLE 9

PERCENTAGE OF CHILDREN IN EACH STREAM WHOSE FATHERS
WERE DEAD, MISSING, IN PRISON OR MENTALLY ILL

	'A'	'B'	'C'	'D'
Two Stream Schools	0.1%	0.7%	—	—
Three Stream Schools	0.5%	0.5%	1.0%	—
Four Stream Schools	0.5%	0.5%	0.5%	2.3%

Those with the least fortunate home were placed in the lowest stream.[2]

There were other kinds of related information I would have liked to collect, such as the family size of pupils in various streams,[3] but I left it out for fear of increasing the refusal rate.

[1] They also illustrate one of the generous sides of streaming: quite consistently a place in a lower stream means a desk in a smaller school class, a larger share of attention from whoever is teaching that class. In table 8, for example, equal sized classes would mean 25 per cent. of the pupils being in the 'A' class and 25 per cent. in the 'D' class. In fact the 'A' classes take more—30 per cent.—and the 'D' classes much less—17 per cent. See page 100 for some clues as to who teaches 'A' classes and who teaches 'D' classes.

[2] In *The Home and The School* (p. 41) Douglas, J. W. B. shows that the children of unemployed fathers can have their chances of passing 11-plus cut by 50 per cent. There is no special element of inherited subnormality to take into account with his figures.

[3] References given on page 138 strongly suggest that children with small families would tend to be in the 'A' streams, children with large families in the low stream—irrespective of social class.

I would also have liked to study more closely the kind of child who changed streams, and how teachers chose them. But the small pilot survey had made it clear to me that they would resist the request for much of this information.

Streaming and birthday

Many teachers must know that streaming works as a form not only of *academic* but of *social* selection, though frequent discussion of the 'classless' grammar school, etc., suggests that not everyone agrees. Are there any other forms of selection that the individual teacher less easily perceives?

Whilst working as a 'B' stream teacher I had once read a short note in *Education*[1] by the Headmaster of a large primary school in Scunthorpe. In his school 74 children had gained grammar school places during the previous two years. But when he graded the children according to birthday he discovered that roughly twice as many (34) had been born during the autumn term as had been born during the summer term (16). Tracing this back he found that the same inequality of birthdays existed between the 'A' stream and the 'C' stream. The ratio of children born in the first four months of the school year, to children born in the remaining eight months, was 100 to 124 in the 'A' stream but 100 to 334 in the 'C' stream.

I was puzzled by this odd report. I had never myself as 'A', 'B' or 'C' teacher noticed any difference in age between the classes. One ten year old girl looked much like another, and whereas I could usually tell the difference between a boy of eight and a boy of nine, my eye was certainly not subtle enough to distinguish the usual child of 10.3 years from the child of 10.6 years.

On reflection it seems there are two related reasons why children born in the winter might more often enter the 'A' stream, and therefore pass the eleven plus than children born in the summer. Firstly, the school class today is usually based on the year group. Eileen may have been born in September and Janet in the following August—and yet quite possibly they are in the same class at school. One child may be almost one year older than another when at the age of six or seven or eight they are

1 Pape, G. V., 'Accident of Birth', *Education*, 16th November, 1956.

streamed, and the road to grammar school opens. In adult life the 'advantage' of a twelve-month may be negligible, but at this early age it means that Eileen has *one seventh* more experience of life than Janet.

The second reason is that children *begin* school at the beginning of any term. But ever afterwards they are promoted as a year group only at the end of the summer term.

They are transferred to the junior school at the end of the school year in which they reach the age of seven. In the extreme instance this can mean that those with birthdays between September and December may have had *three* years in the infants, whereas some of the children born in June and July may have only had *two years*. Again this is only a tiny portion of an adult's life, but it means that one child may have had *fifty per cent.* more experience of school than another when the time comes to grade them both as 'A', 'B', or 'C'.

In the questionnaire therefore the teachers were asked to record the number of children in each school class whose birthdays were between:

1. September 1st and December 31st   (32%)
2. January 1st and April 30th   (34%)
3. May 1st and August 31st   (34%)

The United Kingdom birth rate is spread fairly evenly over these dates, the figures in brackets giving the distribution in the year these children were born. There is no great difference between the spread of births to working class and to middle class mothers.[1]

---

[1] There has been speculation on the subject of whether children born in certain months are intrinsically more intelligent than others. Fitt, A. B., *Seasonal Influence on Growth, Function and Inheritance,* (1941) suggests that children, in the southern hemisphere, born between June and October are on average slightly taller and heavier, and have an average advantage of $1\frac{1}{4}$ I.Q. points. He makes suggestions of an endocrine rhythm and considers possible relationships with hibernation in animals. Frazer Roberts, J. A., 'Intelligence and Season of Conception' in the *British Medical Journal,* 1944, vol. 1, p. 320 is impatient with hypotheses such as 'the higher metabolic level of parental protoplasmic vigour during winter cold seems to be transmitted through the germ-plasm, and to exert a lasting effect upon the future course of the offspring.' He himself advances evidence from a sample of children born in Bath between 1921 and 1925 that May to October children are slightly more intelligent than November to April children. He says that this is the result of intelligent parents choosing to have children in those months. It is however difficult to see why intelligent

But in the two stream school an odd inequality emerges:

TABLE 10

BIRTHDAYS OF 11 YEAR OLD CHILDREN IN 40 TWO-STREAM SCHOOLS

Children born between	*'A' stream*	*'B' stream*
September 1st and December 31st	35%	28%
January 1st and April 30th	33%	34%
May 1st and August 31st	32%	38%
Total %	100%	100%

More children born between September and December found their way into the 'A' stream, whereas the summer-born children tended to be graded as 'B'.

As the number of streams in the schools increases, so does the difference between winter children and summer children. In schools of three, four or five streams the winter-born children slowly gain ground and summer-born sink more and more into 'B', 'C', 'D' and 'E' streams.

Once the unstreamed group is divided into 'A' and 'B', the age advantage within a class and the longer experience in the infant department considerably aids the child born at the lucky time. An apparently slight and fortuitous environmental factor,

---

women should wish to 'carry' their babies during the hot summer months. His results could possibly be explained by the fact that his smaller families tended slightly to be in the May-October group. But as was pointed out in subsequent correspondence in the *British Medical Journal*, his analysis has completely ignored the influence of the school year in Bath. These questions are raised again by Orme, J. E., 'Intelligence, Season of Birth and Climate Temperature' in *British Journal of Psychology* vol. 54 part 3 where a sample of 228 mentally sub-normal patients yielded I.Q. scores related to the trend of the climate throughout their mothers' pregnancies. The suggestion here was that slightly more intelligent children were born in the summer. Whatever subtle truths there may be behind these intriguing speculations, it seems clear that the gross differences dealt with in this chapter are the effect of school and neither planning nor climate. In education authorities with a slightly altered school year, other results were found. For example, Huddersfield calculated August as being for administrative purposes at the beginning, not the end of the school year: consequently the August children there appeared to be rather more successful instead of rather less successful.

unconnected with innate ability, has considerable influence in deciding the child's future in the primary school and later. In the four-stream school almost twice as many summer-born as winter-born children enter the 'D' stream. The situation is more extreme in the small number of 'E', 'F' and 'G' streams investigated.

TABLE 11

BIRTHDAYS OF 11 YEAR OLD CHILDREN IN
252 THREE-STREAM SCHOOLS

Children born between	'A' stream	'B' stream	'C' stream
September 1st and December 31st	38%	30%	25%
January 1st and April 30th	34%	34%	34%
May 1st and August 31st	28%	36%	41%
Total %	100%	100%	100%

TABLE 12

BIRTHDAYS OF 11 YEAR OLD CHILDREN IN
228 FOUR-STREAM SCHOOLS

Children born between	'A' stream	'B' stream	'C' stream	'D' stream
September 1st and December 31st	39%	30%	28%	22%
January 1st and April 30th	35%	37%	33%	36%
May 1st and August 31st	26%	33%	39%	42%
Total %	100%	100%	100%	100%

Does it matter when children are streamed?

If the child's month of birth and his father's occupation have so much to do with a place in the 'A' stream or the 'C' stream, does it matter whether the child is streamed at seven or not until nine? Could it be that these environmental disadvantages count

26

a lot in schools that stream seven year old children, but not so much in schools that wait until the ninth or tenth birthday?

It was possible to compare the birthdays of children who were streamed 'A', 'B' or 'C' at 7 in 56 three-stream schools with some who were streamed at 8, 9 and 10 in 17 similar schools. Table 13 sets this out:

TABLE 13

1. STREAMED AT 7: BIRTHDAYS OF 11 YEAR OLD CHILDREN IN
56 THREE-STREAM SCHOOLS

Children born between	*'A' stream*	*'B' stream*	*'C' stream*
September 1st and December 31st	38%	30%	25%
January 1st and April 30th	35%	35%	35%
May 1st and August 31st	27%	35%	40%
Total%	100%	100%	100%

Compare these with 17 three-stream schools who streamed children at 8, 9 or 10:

TABLE 14

2. STREAMED AT 8, 9 OR 10: BIRTHDAYS OF 11 YEAR OLD
CHILDREN IN 17 THREE-STREAM SCHOOLS

Children born between	*'A' stream*	*'B' stream*	*'C' stream*
September 1st and December 31st	36%	30%	26%
January 1st and April 30th	35%	35%	34%
May 1st and August 31st	29%	35%	40%
Total%	100%	100%	100%

The differences are extremely slight. Both 'B' streams are the same and it is only on the extreme wings of the 'A' classes that there is any difference. In the schools streaming early, only 27 per cent. of the summer children reached the 'A' class; in the schools streaming later, it is 29 per cent. Whether the streaming was early or late the birth-date handicap was still there and still severe.

'Late' streaming produced very similar results to 'early' streaming. I wondered next whether the various methods used for classifying boys and girls as 'A's or 'D's (intelligence or reading tests etc.) changed the picture much. It is clear that in themselves some of the tests used by teachers are very much inferior to others: no 'school reading test' can hope to have the precision and objectivity of the Schonell Graded Word Reading Test. Yet when it came to streaming it didn't seem to matter what methods were included—Schonell tests, 'school tests' or just plain hunch— the same *kind* of children went into 'A' streams or 'D' streams in almost identical proportions. The middle-class winter-born child who did well on a good test, did well on an inferior test.

There was only one exception to this. Results from schools which used intelligence scores were a little different. It was possible to make a small comparison. Table 15 shows what happened to children born between September and December who went to 30 three-stream schools using intelligence tests, compared with children who went to 42 three-stream schools *not* using them.

TABLE 15

THE EFFECT OF INTELLIGENCE TESTS ON THE STREAMING OF
AUTUMN-BORN CHILDREN

Type of School	'A' stream	'B' stream	'C' stream	Total %
30 Schools using Intelligence Tests	44%	33%	23%	100%
42 Schools *not* using Intelligence Tests	47%	33%	20%	100%

But in schools using intelligence tests only 44 per cent. of the autumn children went into the 'A' stream, whereas in other schools it was 47 per cent. The use of intelligence tests had a very mild equalising effect, possibly in part because such tests include an age weighting. But they also had a very similar effect on the social composition of the various streams.[1]

Summary

A sample of 660 primary schools showed that 96 per cent. used some form of streaming, and that most did this when the children were 7, though there were examples of it at younger ages. A third of the schools used no objective test in helping them. A number of teachers questioned much underestimated the present-day extent of streaming.

When analysed by social background, it was clear that streaming worked as a major form of social as well as academic selection. There were only 5 chances in 100 of a professional's or manager's child going into a 'D' class. It also partly divided children according to their date of birth. 'D' streams had twice as many summer-born as winter-born children. All this remained true whether streaming took place early or later, and whatever tests the school used didn't affect the kind of children who became 'A', 'B' or 'C'. The exception was that the use of standardised intelligence tests had a slight equalising effect.

Suppose, for the sake of speculation, that the trend of summer-born children from working-class homes moving into the lowest stream remained consistent. This means that if someone built a primary school with 18 streams somewhat bigger than a large comprehensive school, then no child in the 'R' stream would have a middle-class father. Neither would any of them be born before May or later than August. Probably a large number would be those who most needed the help school could give them—children from fatherless or broken homes, children whose fathers were imprisoned, unemployed, crippled or ill.

[1] Since the above was written two Local Authorities, Durham and Yorkshire West Riding have carried out independent local enquiries of their own. Durham's findings confirm that streaming divides children up according to their birthday, and also shows that when Heads recommend pupils for grammar school places they tend to select the winter-born children again. The Durham information indicates that this handicap has a noticeable effect on the child's secondary school stream and can even be seen in G.C.E. 'O' level results. When 218 G.C.E. candidates from seven secondary modern schools were analysed, 101 had birthdays between September 1st and December 31st and only 48 between May 1st and August 31st. In the West Riding the Education Committee minutes say that evidence has been received that winter born children are taking more than their expected proportion of 'A' stream places, but no figures are quoted.

This is an extreme fantasy. It is based on the evidence here that streaming builds on a range of environmental handicaps —some of which can have no connection with native endowment—and translates them into academic grades. Those gradings—'A', 'B' or 'C'—are for many children a statement of their life chances.

I had seen little of this as a primary school teacher myself. When I was happily teaching *Sir Patrick Spens* or less happily struggling with Rivers of Africa, I had only a mild sense of the social composition of the class. I knew little about the children's homes, their months of birth, their family size, their father's work and education. I didn't think about children in that way. I knew their classroom selves too well, I was too close to the detail of their personalities to see the kind of facts I have tried to tabulate here. Very many primary teachers must feel as I did. And in that situation, so very much on top of the children all day long, it is tempting to account for individual differences largely in terms of heredity.

I know very little about the genetic bases of human skills.[1] So far as I can see the evidence as to whether a greater proportion of intelligent children are born in middle-class rather than working-class homes is inconclusive. I certainly accept as a reasonable assumption that there is some genetic base ultimately determining a child's potential achievements. Whether it is distributed at random or not, I do not know. But it seems fruitless to 'play off' environment against heredity. Current research is continually pushing back the popular frontiers of 'heredity', showing how much more than we expected can be accounted for by environment, how much more complex the inter-relation of nature and nurture proves to be. In this study I am therefore assuming, but leaving aside the importance of heredity. I think it is there, but I think we are a vast way yet from perceiving and removing environmental handicaps. The genetic limits to human excellence are a practical problem for a later age than ours.

[1] A neat summary of environment and heredity as it effects early selection is to be found in *Procedures for the Allocation of Pupils in Secondary Education* (NFER, 1963).

3

WHAT THE TEACHERS WROTE

I KNEW a little about streaming from personal experience. I had discovered a certain amount about the situation in some six hundred large primary schools. As a teacher the question presented itself to me in one way, as a research worker it looked different. How, I wondered, did other teachers see streaming—not the teachers who write articles and appear on TV, but the great body of primary school men and women who have their say in staff room and classroom, but seldom in print or on the air. To get some idea of this I attached an 'opinion' section to the questionnaire analyzed in the last chapter. It was completed by 655 teachers, of whom all but 24 taught in stream schools.[1] 217 of the replies came from Heads and 438 from class teachers. All of them were first asked whether, in general, they favoured streaming or not. Eighty five per cent. did favour it, 9 per cent. were hostile to it, and 6 per cent. held mixed views. The larger the school the more the staff liked streaming. But the strongest supporters of all were teachers who took 'C' streams (91 per cent. in favour). Head teachers were slightly less ready to support it than class teachers, but these differences were small. On this sample support for streaming was overwhelming from every type of teacher and school.

This chapter is going to be largely concerned with the majority of teachers who favoured streaming. This is partly because I have far more evidence from this group, and partly because I am particularly interested in them. I suspect they represent the largest but least articulate group in primary schools. Politicians may maintain or abolish 11 plus, 12 plus or 13 plus, but it is these teachers who create the classroom situation. Their

---

[1] Five of the 660 schools returning questionnaires did not complete this section. All 5 objected to the questions on Fathers' occupation.

way of looking at children may have a vast, immeasurable influence. So far as I can I have presented them commenting on education. Not quite, for postal questionnaires are crude and I am sure 618 face-to-face interviews, besides giving more information about who the teachers were, would have produced more downright talking; filling in a questionnaire has probably diluted and oversimplified their opinions. But such interviews were beyond my resources.

Why do we Stream?

What did the teachers claim as the major purposes of streaming? The 85 per cent. who favoured streaming were invited to select prime purposes from a list of five commonly mentioned ones; or to add others of their own. The five common reasons and the percentage of teachers choosing each are set out below. One teacher could choose several purposes if he wished, so the figures do not total 100 per cent.

TEACHERS FAVOURING STREAMING

A prime purpose of streaming is to help the less gifted child	95%
A prime purpose of streaming is to help the gifted child	88%
A prime purpose of streaming is to help in making teaching easier	44%
A prime purpose of streaming is to maintain good 11-plus standards	12%
A prime purpose of streaming is to simplify school organisation	11%

The first and second purposes were usually combined (i.e. streaming meets the need of *all* children). The basic claim is that though streaming helps the gifted child, and though some acknowledge convenience and 11-plus standards as a prime purpose, it is above all as a device to help the less gifted child that streaming is practical.

In 1961 the average primary school class had 32 children. There were 6,970 in schools with classes of 51 or more. Could it be that teachers (especially class teachers) supported streaming because it was a sensible way of handling large numbers? Exactly one third introduced the subject of large classes into their case for streaming. Teachers who were undecided about streaming had large classes much in mind (44 per cent.), whereas teachers who were against streaming mentioned these conditions rather less (27 per cent.). So although large classes played some part in these answers, more was at work.

The nine per cent. who were against streaming did not agree:

TEACHERS HOSTILE TO STREAMING

A prime purpose of streaming is to help the gifted child	63%
A prime purpose of streaming is to make teaching easier	63%
A prime purpose of streaming is to help the less gifted child	50%
A prime purpose of streaming is to maintain good 11-plus standards	44%
A prime purpose of streaming is to simplify school organisation	22%

And the undecided teachers concurred with this second order, except in one respect: they also promoted the education of the less gifted child from third to first place. Few teachers added any further reasons.

Is this a reliable insight into teachers' reasons for and against streaming? Obviously there is something real here, for the one group of teachers is primarily claiming that streaming is for the benefit of the weaker child, whereas the other group chiefly contends that it is for the benefit of the 'A' stream child and for the teacher ('to make teaching easier'). But it could be that these answers were blurred by the choice of 'correct' responses, of 'public' rather than 'private' answers.

Different ones might have been obtained if the five reasons had not been printed on the questionnaire. These doubts are suggested because the answers to the next questions are somewhat inconsistent with the previous ones.

If your school were unstreamed . . .

The teachers favouring streaming were asked how they thought staff and pupils would be affected if the school were *unstreamed*. What, for example, would happen to the morale of 'A' stream teachers?

33

What the Teachers Wrote

Some thought this was an absurd question:

'Is there such a thing as an 'A' stream teacher?'

Headteacher, Middlesbrough

'Teachers constantly change stream. I cannot see the relevance of the question.'

Headteacher, Wallasey

'Rubbish.'

Headteacher, Kent

Almost half claimed that morale would be unchanged:

'A ridiculous question. Teachers are paid to teach. Their morale should not be altered.'

Headteacher, Plymouth

'A poor question. Teachers are teachers of children, not of any particular stream.'

Headteacher, Kent

'Not applicable to a dedicated teacher.'

'A' stream teacher, Hampshire

But nearly 40 per cent. of those favouring streaming said morale would drop:

'Shattered!'

'C' stream teacher, Shropshire

'They would leave the school.'

'A' stream teacher, West Riding

'Teachers over 45 would resent it, as promotion to Headship now very unlikely (saddled forever!).'

Headteacher, Kent

'Under present conditions, and aiming for 11-plus, there would be frustration.'

'A' stream teacher, Birmingham

'Morale down, because what many theorists fail to realise is that there are 'A', 'B' and 'C' teachers in the same way as there are 'A', 'B' and 'C' children.'

Headteacher, Coventry

Only 2 per cent. believed morale would rise:

'Should make them return to the basic principles of education.'
Headteacher, Essex

'Might be more ready to realise the individual differences amongst children.'
'B' stream teacher, Nottingham

And what of the morale of 'B' and 'C' teachers? Again the largest group expected no change for exactly the same reasons as previously illustrated. But this time 21 per cent. of those favouring streaming, nevertheless said morale would *rise*:

'Would be relieved from the monotony of teaching children of low ability.'
'A' stream teacher, Hull

'Much improved. Many of the public openly say "She's only a 'C' teacher".'
'C' stream teacher, Shropshire

'Enchanted, as they would reap greater rewards.'
'C' stream teacher, West Riding

Only 10 per cent. foresaw that morale would *drop*:

'Those who teach less gifted children are either dedicated or lack the drive of the 'A' stream teacher.'
'A' stream teacher, Croydon

'Many have taken special courses for 'C' stream work. They might feel their trouble wasted, and some specialists would suffer financially.'
Headteacher, Warwick

'Many 'C' stream teachers would not feel competent to teach children who are often brighter than themselves.'
Headteacher, Huddersfield

So although only 3 per cent. of the low stream teachers had been against streaming, 22 per cent. of them felt their spirits would rise if 'B' and 'C' streams were abolished. Either they were more undecided than appeared at a first glance, or one of these two questions was touching the nerves, and not the official surface. Certainly the quotations indicate shrewd sense, as well as revealing some of the interests, ambitions, and differing values concealed by the percentages.

It was mostly teachers in smaller schools who claimed morale would rise. No-one at all in a four-stream school claimed the 'A' teacher would feel better. The explanation may be that a teacher in an AB school is accustomed to handling 50 per cent. of the normal ability range in one classroom; the teacher in an A B C D E school usually teaches only a 20 per cent. ability range. The two-stream teacher may be somewhat more convinced that a 100 per cent. ability range could be taught in one classroom—and that he could do it.

Many teachers had contended that the teacher's morale either didn't matter, or would be unchanged. It was the children who mattered and were affected. Which children? And in what ways? To begin with, what impact would unstreaming make on the academic standard of the children's work?

Ninety one per cent. of the teachers favouring streaming said standards would drop:

'Slump!'

'C' stream teacher, Newcastle

'Lower. Bad money drives out good.'

'A' stream teacher, Essex

'Definitely suffer; and as intelligence is one of our few remaining raw materials, this would be a tragedy.'

Headteacher, Hartlepool

But which children in particular would 'slump'—the gifted, or the less gifted? Eighty three per cent. said the work of the gifted child would suffer—headteachers and 'A' stream teachers both feeling more strongly on this point than other teachers.

'We need to remove the gifted from a class far more often than we do.'

Headteacher, Birmingham

'The gifted are always the most neglected children in school. We hear of classes for the backward—why not special classes for the very bright children? Genius languishes in the doldrums.'

Headteacher, Wiltshire

'There would be the danger of putting a gifted child to help a less gifted one.'

'A' stream teacher, Smethwick

On the other hand the percentage of teachers who felt that the work of the less gifted would suffer, dropped to 75 per cent. In two-stream schools it was even lower—51 per cent. Since these teachers had previously claimed that streaming was primarily designed to benefit the less gifted child, it seems surprising that relatively so many of them accept that unstreaming would academically either not affect or possibly benefit such children. But whereas they are clearly in two minds about this, they remain single-minded about the results of unstreaming on the 'A' stream child.

Nevertheless, the majority saw a black future:

'The backward child will be emotionally bewildered by the daily evidence of differing capabilities.'

Headteacher, Kent

'The poorer the home, the more stupid the child. These children from poor homes grow up together, play together, and accept working together.'

'A' stream teacher, Birmingham

Of course there are other elements in the classroom than the teacher's morale, or the standard of the children's work. Discipline is a subject important to teachers: how might that be affected by unstreaming?

Sixty per cent. expected no difference on the grounds that:

'Discipline is a matter of "tone" set by the headmaster and staff. Whether the school is streamed or not should not affect it.'

Headteacher, Kent

And this time only 31 per cent. felt discipline would deteriorate:

'Two or three troublesome children can upset the working atmosphere essential to 'A' stream children.'

'E' stream teacher, Essex

'I would concede that the 'C' stream toughs would be broken down into smaller cells, but they would still gang up.'

Headteacher, Leicester

Finally what of the children's social attitudes?

37

D

Again over half (56 per cent.) expected no change:

'Not affected. I don't have to go drinking with my dustman although he may be considered my equal. So with children.'

Headteacher, Leicester

'Little difference. Lot of bunkum talked by long-haired intellectuals in this field.'

'A' stream teacher, Bedford

Eighteen per cent. foresaw a change for the worse:

'Chaotic.'

'B' stream teacher, Manchester

'I generally find ill-mannered children harm good ones.'

Headteacher, Sunderland

'In lower class areas, a general lowering.'

'A' stream teacher, Cardiff

But this time 26 per cent. actually thought that social attitudes would *improve*:

'Rather strangely this is an argument against streaming. I have found 'B' classes much more untidy, much more noisy and more irresponsible than 'A' classes. On moving children from one to the other there has been a marked improvement, and vice versa.'

Headteacher, Birmingham

What can be made of these guesses at the future? The particular forecasts compare oddly with the previous table on general sentiments about the purpose of streaming.

TABLE 16

IF SCHOOLS WERE UNSTREAMED ...

	Worse	*Better*
Academic Standards	91%	2%
The gifted child	83%	5%
Less gifted child	75%	12%
Morale of 'A' stream staff	40%	2%
Discipline	31%	9%
Social attitudes	18%	26%
Morale of 'B' stream staff	10%	21%

In their general statements the claim is that streaming is primarily designed to help the 'B' or 'C' stream child; in their particular comments they show themselves as rather more concerned with the effects of unstreaming on academic standards—particularly those of the 'A' stream child. Some even believe that children's social attitudes are worse in a streamed school, and the morale of 'B' and 'C' stream staff lower. The education they defend is one which never loses sight of the duty of schools to impress good academic skills, though in hard daily practice, other 'social' aspects of education may sometimes have to be put aside. The sternest defenders of these concepts were class teachers in large establishments, the least sure were the headteachers of two-stream schools. Throughout the answers ran a slightly defensive tone as if many teachers were conscious that the principle of streaming was being challenged.

Who are the critics of streaming?

From where does the attack on streaming come? Twelve possible sources were offered to the teachers, and they were asked to choose the groups who were sceptical of streaming—or to add other ones of their own. Thirteen per cent. of the teachers favouring streaming refused to answer this or the next question, either because they disliked the method used—

'This is pure hearsay and we will have nothing to do with it.'
Headteacher, West Riding

Or because they did not believe in sociology—

'There are no such things as groups or group opinions.'
'B' stream teacher, Ipswich

Or because it inflated the whole question—

'Studying your list of choices, my thoughts wander far, far beyond streaming—so much so that I wonder if you are not making a lot out of such a small thing. My parents simply accept my judgment.'
Headteacher, Croydon

Or because the question did not exist—

'I have been a Headmaster for 30 years, and have never heard of any scepticism about streaming.'
Headmaster, Nottingham

The remaining 87 per cent. of the teachers who favoured streaming located the opposition as follows. Again teachers could choose several types of critic, so the figures do not total 100 per cent.

TABLE 17

WHO IS SCEPTICAL ABOUT STREAMING?

People in education who are *not* practising teachers	61%
People with a chip on their shoulder	49%
Parents of children in low streams	49%
People of left-wing sympathies	36%
Lesser-educated people	23%
Middle-class parents	18%
Inexperienced teachers	16%
Teachers of 'B' or 'C' classes	9%
Very experienced teachers	7%
Working class parents	6%
Teachers of 'A' classes	3%
People with right wing sympathies	2%
Total Number	538

The only one of these choices which alters much according to the size of the school is 'parents of children in low streams'. They were felt as a major challenge in two-stream schools (59 per cent.), but a minor one in four-stream schools (37 per cent.). This is hardly surprising since we have seen from previous analyses that the social grading of the streaming process means that children in the 'E' stream of a five-stream school will have the least vocal parents, whereas 32 per cent. of the middle-class children are in the 'B' stream of a two-stream school.

Teachers added very few new groups to the list above. Several times there was a comment along these lines:

'In this area it is the parents who are rising in the social scale, or keeping up with the Joneses, who feel the social stigma if their child is in a lower stream than their neighbours.'

Headteacher, Cheshire

And another new group was certainly defined with considerable vigour:

'Headteachers who want to please certain Inspectors.'

Headteacher, Cumberland

'Teachers who find non-streaming a useful gimmick to bring themselves to an Inspector's notice, with a view to promotion.'
'A' stream teacher, Yorkshire

'Teachers who care more about starting new fashions than the welfare of the children.'
Headteacher, Hampshire

'Teachers after publicity.'
Headteacher, Huddersfield

But most often the teachers wished to emphasise or expand the choice they had made. 'People who are *not* practising teachers' was vigorously underlined, heavily ticked, or warmly commented on:

'Earnest reformers with no background who are disposed to accept slogans and emotionalism.'
Headteacher, Lancashire

'Extremists who pay homage to the idea of equal opportunity.'
'A' stream teacher, Warwick

'Amateurs trying to tell us what to do. Education is the only profession at which everyone thinks he is an expert.'
'B' stream teacher, Southport

'The cranks of this world.'
'B' stream teacher, Plymouth

'Ivory towered lecturers in education.'
'C' stream teacher, Stoke

'People who have studied at length the Apes and the Monkeys, and have been rewarded by Education Authorities treating them as CHILD experts.'
'B' stream teacher, Leeds

'These sociologists with no practical experience.'
'B' stream teacher, Birmingham

'People looking for research to do. Otherwise there is no feeling on this subject.'
Headteacher, Kent

Psychologists, sociologists, school inspectors, local councillors, vicars, journalists, training college lecturers all came under heavy attack. Many teachers insisted on expanding their choices by adding practical considerations:

41

'These ill-informed critics do not realise the amount of work that would be necessary in preparing and marking work for an unstreamed class: it would virtually be 3 or 4 small classes.'

'A' stream teacher, Essex

'Streaming *must* bring home to parents the comparative abilities of their children. Sometimes this comes as a shock and a disappointment, but I don't find they blame the system which reveals this information to them.'

Headteacher, Derby

Or by adding social comment:

'The one disadvantage of streaming is that parents (the non-intelligent type) feel that a child is condemned for life if he doesn't make the 'A' stream. Only if the parents got full information from the school will these fears subside.'

Headteacher, Norwich

'I feel that one of the causes of social disorder today is this supposition that all are equal.'

Headteacher, Blackpool

Who defends streaming?

The same teachers were then presented with the opposite question, and asked to indicate or add groups whom they felt supported streaming.

TABLE 18
WHO FAVOURS STREAMING?

Very experienced teachers	73%
Teachers of 'A' classes	53%
Teachers of 'B' and 'C' classes	35%
Middle-class parents	31%
People with right wing sympathies	15%
Working-class parents	9%
Parents with children in low streams	9%
Inexperienced teachers	8%
People in education who are *not* practising teachers	6%
People with left wing sympathies	2%
Lesser educated people	2%
People with a chip on their shoulder	1%
Total number	538

Whereas they had chiefly seen criticism of streaming as coming from outside the school, they were fairly confident that their greatest support lay in their fellow teachers—especially the very experienced, and the 'A' stream teachers. From our previous analysis we know that they may be slightly mistaken here, and that 'C' stream teachers may be even stronger proponents of streaming.

Once more teachers frequently added comment after their choices:

'In my experience streaming gives middle-class children the chance that their parents had in private or prep. schools, now that the state schools are more widely used.'

'A' stream teacher, Stockport

'Most parents—middle-class and working-class—accept streaming. The only ones who are not content to leave the placing of the child to us are some parents who think that the so-called 'A' class means a near-certain pass. We have proved this to be wrong only this year, when 4 out of the 'B' class of 41 passed, and 2 out of the 'A' class of 45 failed. Some benefit by being top of the 'B' class and not bottom of the 'A' class, as we have shown.'

Headteacher, Birmingham

And here again, as at so many points in the questioning, were the remarks pointing out that streaming was the private concern of the teaching profession, or alternatively, a matter of little consequence to anybody.

'It doesn't seem to me that streaming is the concern of groups in society other than teachers. Streaming hasn't anything to do with anything—except efficiency in teaching.'

Headteacher, Northampton

'Nobody doubts the rightness of streaming. They simply want their child to be in the 'A' stream.'

'A' stream teacher, Warwickshire

'No one seems to worry.'

'A' stream teacher, Birmingham

This chapter has considered one of the most crucial facts in the classroom situation. In determining which children shall develop along the 'A', 'B' or 'C' paths, it may be that teachers' opinions on streaming are even more important than the childrens' social class or date of birth. The overwhelming majority of these teachers wanted streaming, and had no difficulty in defining their position. In their view streaming made teaching less arduous and served the needs of all children. It advanced high academic standards, especially in the 'A' stream, and realistically made plain to children and parents the inevitable differences between one pupil's ability and another's. They believed that those who knew classroom conditions at first hand supported the principle, and that such criticism as there was came from outside the schools, particularly from people in education who were at one remove from the actual teaching. Considering that they were presenting their views in writing, and often forwarding them to me via their Education Office, most teachers seemed perfectly candid and vigorous in recording their position. Very many times they added long comments arguing that streaming could not be considered in isolation, or regarded merely as a teaching technique. A few claimed the opposite, but for most teachers it was one expression of a philosophy of education, or a reflection of a process of natural selection and competition that could not, or should not, be challenged.

'From a Head's point of view the whole situation can be made much worse by allowing parents to gather in large numbers and talk, such as in Parent-Teacher Associations. Such gossip arouses inter-parental jealousy, which over-rides commonsense. Therefore to avoid difficulties, keep parents apart. Many of this type of parent have come from a working-class background. There is a fear that the child's failure to make the 'A' stream will affect their status in relation to their fellow workers where, in a dull envy-ridden community, even the opportunity to "crow" is denied them. The whole principle of streaming has been developed in the English educational system to give the greatest efficiency from the resources of teachers, buildings and equipment available. Some other examples would be:

Oxford and Cambridge *versus* the rest of the universities.
Honours courses *versus* ordinary degree courses.
Grammar schools *versus* secondary modern schools.
Modern schools with GCE courses *versus* Modern schools with non-GCE courses.
Comprehensive schools, where streaming is hidden but very real.

I fail to see why a system which has proved efficient and accept-able in all other levels of education should suddenly become suspect and immoral at the primary stage.'

Headmaster, Lancashire

'Throughout industry it is necessary to grade products.'

'C' stream teacher, London

'There are two types of children, those who want to work and those who don't, the same as in adult life.'

Headteacher, Leicester

'In the training of racehorses and athletes we are most careful to cream, train, and cream again. Why not with children?'

'B' stream teacher, West Hartlepool

'Not to stream in a large junior school would be the height of professional irresponsibility.'

Headteacher, Lincoln

Finally, it must be recorded that here and there teachers' comments showed that there were some amongst the supporters of streaming who might qualify their view in different circum-stances, or were conscious of problems that they had not solved.

'I favour streaming, but I wouldn't apply it to the 5-plus age group.'

'B' stream teacher, North Riding

'If a realistic alternative could be put forward I would be delighted and relieved. But, without being unfair to the brighter element in the bitter contest for grammar school places, I cannot see one.'

'A' stream teacher, Birmingham

'With extremely small classes, e.g. 12 to 16 pupils, another situa-tion arises.'

'A' stream teacher, Northamptonshire

'I would be happier if streaming was more fluid, but promoting one child from the 'B' class means sending down another from the 'A'. The better group in the 'B' class doesn't work to maxi-mum capacity, probably because of the lack of stimulus from a few 'A' children. This is one of the problems I have not solved.

Another factor which worries me is the "gap" between 'A' stream attainments and those of my 'B' stream. There is some slight overlap in the first year of the school, but by the fourth year there is such a wide gap that it cannot be crossed.'

Headmaster, Hereford

This chapter has presented teachers' opinions, largely those of teachers favouring streaming. My own guess is that the teachers about whom we hear most—those who are quoted in print and over the air—may not represent the bulk of the primary school profession. I suspect that the quotations given here tell us a little about those of whom we know least—and who are yet the majority, and as influential as any when it comes to the kind of boys and girls that these schools help to shape.

The questionnaire method on which this evidence is based is rather limited. I now wanted to have a look at some of these teachers in action and study one streamed school in detail. I therefore picked out the schools within travelling distance for me which had returned questionnaires, and asked the Education Officers for permission to visit them. The first Education Officer I approached told me that one of the schools about which I had enquired was the very best streamed school in his area. This school was called Honey Bell.

4

HONEY BELL:
A STREAMED SCHOOL

HONEY BELL Primary school straddles the summit of a
small hill. Long clean blocks of glass and cedar-wood
radiate from the central building, and the sheer glass
face of the tall main block glistens for miles in the spring sunlight. Down below wavering shafts of light, reflected from the
swimming pool, play rapidly across the dark wood sections.
The first time I went there I remember watching a small boy in
a red wool jumper come out of a large glass door, and breaking
into half a run and half a dance, race and prance across the
surrounding football pitches, and then disappear into the cricket
pavilion. Beyond the pavilion is a suburban road.

Honey Bell school is in one of England's new towns. None of
the thousands of houses surrounding the school—a delightful
variety of white wood, dark wood, grey brick, blue brick, red
brick and white brick—are more than ten years old. The school
itself superbly dominates the neighbourhood; and from the flat
roof of the main block, the towers of other schools, flashing in
the sunlight, stand out at even intervals among the great acres
of two-storey housing. The schools, like castles in the mediaeval
countryside or the white steeples of Wren churches in Caroline
London, are the architectural images which match most nearly
the life around. This is a town crowded with children.

In the central square of the town, the pool is lined by small
boys and girls; the entrance to Woolworth's blocked by prams
and push chairs, and loud with crying babies. Boys roller skate
round the market stalls, girls cluster round the doll shop windows. Groups of children squeal, climb, hide, and balance on
the forms and benches designed for the tired and the old. They
cycle in bunches around the neighbourhoods, and once I saw a
coal wagon unable to deliver its load because the avenue was

jammed by *tricycles*. No London bus or Sheffield bus is like a bus here. Buses vibrate with excited children. On the top deck, guns, magnifying glasses, chewing gum, notebooks, are all at the ready. Downstairs small children sit on mother's lap and stare, or squirm between her knees and shout.

When the schools open their glass doors and take them in, the town is a different place, and the neighbourhoods, deserted except for adults and toddlers, lose for the moment their special flash and colour. The teachers take over, and educate one of the most vivacious child populations in England, in surroundings splendidly designed and generously equipped. I chose the town, and Honey Bell school because I next wanted to study a streamed school in action. And it seemed wisest to choose a first-class streamed school, and not a shabby one; and one which had been built up in new, pleasant and even lavish surroundings. Honey Bell offered all these to a population which was responding to a new start in life. I met Mr. Rivers, Headmaster of Honey Bell, and for the next six months was in and out of the school.

When I first visited Honey Bell, Mr. Rivers took me on a tour of the buildings. At the entrance to the first playground was a neat painted notice explaining that parents must not pass beyond that point unless they had business with the Headmaster. Beyond this were wide curving paths, trim grass verges, a tall carved totem pole and a brilliantly coloured wigwam, large enough to hold half a dozen children. Pupils had constructed both. By the wigwam was an open air swimming pool. Staff and parents built this themselves. From here we passed between two blocks of classrooms into the main play area. There were climbing frames, a wall to bounce balls against, neat white markings on the asphalt for team games. On the sides away from the school building, the main playground was edged by the school pet-farm, and by cricket and football pitches sloping down to the main road. The pet farm was a rough field full of hutches, wire runs, straying hens and an animal house. The animal house had been built largely by the Headmaster himself, though some of the staff worked on it in the evenings. Constructed of brick, netting and corrugated iron, it has compartments in which birds or animals can be separated by type or stage of growth. There is just room for a class of children to enter, watch, and be sheltered from the rain. As he points out the different breeds of hen, Mr. Rivers is already bending back part of the corrugated roof, clipping up a hole in the wire.

In the animal house, and running freely in the rough, are hens of many sorts—Rhode Island, Peking, silver-spangled Hamburgers. Young chicks are penned together and there are plans afoot to let the children observe for themselves the results of interbreeding. In other boxes, huts or compartments, are weasels, mice, guinea pigs, hamsters, rabbits of several kinds, a peacock and peahen, and a vixen.

Leaving the boys to finish the netting and feed the hens, Mr. Rivers took me across the cricket pitch to the pavilion. Outside, the pavilion looks very new, white and correct. Inside it is not quite finished. There is some plastering and a patch of re-roofing to do. The visitors' changing room has still to be painted, and a set of mural ceramics showing a boy with a football, another with a bat, a girl diving and a girl with a racket, is waiting to be cemented. The pavilion was built by staff and parents, the ceramics made by the children.

We walk back to the school, through the tight glass doors, The doves in the cote above flutter, as always, and settle down again. In the spacious entrance hall there is a large, tiered display stand built by Mr. Rivers. On it are carvings and small pieces of pottery. I can't tell whether they are by teachers or children. On another stand is a grotesque limb from a fallen tree, magnificently burnished. A mobile of tinted cards gyrates above. As the draught steers each card round, one by one they are designed to challenge the young child's imagination—
—*Whose? What? Whence?* Beyond this are open reading shelves and chairs for reference work or library periods. The books are abundant, very new and in excellent condition. Over and above his book allowance, Mr. Rivers is a past master in the art of persuading calling salesmen to leave specimen copies of their best publications. At one end of the hall is a small display of photos and essays on Switzerland, where the teachers recently took one class for a week. On the visitors' chairs outside the Head's study are books showing photographs of the school at work, and examples of prose and poetry—carefully rhymed little verses about spring, holidays, school, snow. Every few minutes a child walks quietly across the hall. Even this is

sufficient to set the mobiles dancing: especially the one directly in every child's path, which reads in turn

> *Have you cleaned your teeth today?*
> *Be tidy*
> *Are you wearing your house badge?*
> *Work hard*
> *Have you a handkerchief?*
> *Be proud of being British*

At the end of the entrance hall are the House shields for different sports and for academic work. Glittering alongside them are the football, cricket, athletic and netball cups that Honey Bell has won in competition against other schools.

Leading off from the entrance hall is the large assembly hall. It is used for morning prayers, physical education, school plays and open days. Near the entrance the school song and the school prayer are pinned on the wall. On the high rostrum where the Headmaster stands is a reading stand with an open Bible. Jumbled in a corner lie tangled coils of climbing ropes, and stored at one end are the units that slot together to make the stage. These were made by the staff. Every time the sunlight flickers on the swimming pool outside waves of blue light sweep through the glass and around the hall. Inside, the most brilliant touch of colour comes from the school crest, and the four house shields mounted above the rostrum. Each house has its symbol, colour and name. The name plates read *Churchill, Hillary, Bader, Schweitzer.*

From the two halls, classrooms and corridors lead off in many directions, so that every room seems a private world within itself. From one you look down on boys and girls splashing in the swimming pool; from another you see the vixen, a third opens onto the cricket pitch, a fourth is slung like a balcony over the playground, with the doves continually fluttering by its windows. Each classroom has its own washbasins and lavatory, and sufficient floor space for art or drama. All have excellent modern furniture.

These are the common features and differences that the architect has given the classrooms. But there are other differences that children and teachers have created. It is simplest to describe the classrooms of the 11 year old children—4A, 4B and

4C. The visible differences between the streams are there, even in the classrooms of 7 year old children, but they become distinctly clearer as the children grow older. During the lunch hour, when the room is deserted, 4A still remains an 'A' classroom. Pinned on the walls are a great many examples of good handwriting and model essays by the children. There is much more children's writing than children's painting. Fastened here and there are hand-printed kerchiefs, newly finished. These are most painstakingly done in patterns of repeated units—squares, triangles, circles, stars. A chequer board design is the favourite, and each must have taken hours of extremely patient, neat, and repetitive industry. In one corner stands a large model of a mediaeval castle. It is painted grey, and its square stones have been carefully hatched in, text book fashion, with pen-and-ink to give the conventional indications for shadow. The castle is crowded with toy soldiers freely brought by the children themselves. Hanging behind the castle are two paintings of the classroom itself, both of which made a strenuous attempt at photographic fidelity. Drying on the window ledge are further tiles to complete the sporting mural in the cricket pavilion.

4B is not at all like this. Even when the children are out it is alive with noise. On open tables running along one wall are boxes, hutches and cages rowdy with hens, hamsters, doves and rabbits. This class is largely responsible for the animal life belonging to the school, and often a cage or hutch will be brought indoors to demonstrate a lesson, or because a bird is sick, or to get ready for a regional display, when the entries from Honey Bell often win awards. It is almost always children from 4B who feed and tend the animals, and they do this excellently. Besides the cages, the walls of 4B are covered with plans and paintings. There is a scale plan of the animal house posted up, and a sketch of the incubator (built by the Head and Mr. Frond, 4B's form master) in which the class watches chickens hatching out. Here and there are other paintings—largely portraits of children and teachers. They are not as patient and careful as the art-work of 4A, but aim at the dash and reality of the lightning portraits you can often see sketched at the seaside. There is a great deal of interest in line work—shading, thickening, hatching—but relatively little in colour or brush. About half the wall is covered by instructions, diagrams, lists, drawn up by the teacher.

4C is different again. It is a smaller and more intimate class-room. Whereas the desks in 4A and 4B were in regular serried ranks facing the teacher's dais, here they are broken into small groups so that children face other children. The distinction of 4C is the quality of its woodwork. The class has made wooden stools, boxes, ships, simple toys. All the woodwork produces practical objects that a ten year old could use, and there is nothing slipshod about the sawing, mortices or nailwork. Girls in 4C were just as good as boys, and except that they made sew-ing boxes instead of tool boxes it would not be easy to tell their work apart. The most striking object on show is a large model of the *Cutty Sark* that class and teacher are building for the school's annual Open Day. Near the teacher's desk stands a circular saw, bought from funds raised by the school and built up by the staff. Because of its obvious hazard only Mr. Wardle, the form-master, and the Head himself use it. About two thirds of the wall is covered with instructions and diagrams by the teacher.

The Headmaster

Clearly the character of the school owes much to the drive and personality of Mr. Rivers, the Headmaster. He is a small, sudden man with a powerful voice that rings through the build-ing. Full of quick energetic gestures he is continually on the move, pouncing on slackness or untidiness, restlessly seeking for improvements. He can be seen striding across the playing fields, mending a broken pipe in the swimming pool, repairing the roof, admiring the knit of a small boy's jumper. Usually there is a knot of teachers or children or officials clustering around him or trailing in his wake. He is now in his mid-forties, and has been (except for his distinguished war service) a Head-master for twenty years.

'When I got my first job as a Head I inherited the worst lot of staff you've ever seen. A dreary set of idlers who'd been mooning on for years and years with the school decaying round them. So the first thing was to get rid of that lot. But when I said that to the Education Officer he replied "You can't do things of that sort." All the same by the end of that term the whole lot except one had resigned. So then I had my pick of the young men coming in from the colleges—that's what you want, ambitious young men, willing to work hard and push ahead. We soon had that school going like a bomb, and cleared the decks of everything.

And I'll tell you this: by and large you don't want to recruit your teachers from Suffolk, Surrey, Essex, Middlesex, Norfolk, Kent, Bedfordshire, Herefordshire, Worcestershire, and certainly not from the L.C.C. I know there are exceptions, but they only prove the rule. Best of all you want keen young men from places like Lancashire and Yorkshire, who'll go after promotion themselves.'

Mr. Rivers has little patience with teachers who leave school at 4 o'clock and have no connection with the neighbourhood, and not much either with genteel daughters of the upper class who descend into teaching as a nice thing to do. He wants men and women who would forge ahead in other jobs, and though the new town is badly short of teachers, Honey Bell school is always fully staffed. Teachers like and respond to the challenge he makes:

'I must have tangible results—the swimming pool, the pavilion, the results. Recently we were keeping the children here up till half past five, quarter to six. What were they doing? Playing hockey, doing woodwork, learning French. Yes, French —and then some people said it was to give them an advantage in the 11-plus. Can you imagine any more wicked clap-trap than that?'

On joining the staff, the new teacher is given a letter introducing him to the standards expected in the school. Manners and appearance are to be carefully watched:

'Regular inspections of children should take place for:
    (a)   Shoes
    (b)   Hair-partings, etc.
    (c)   Handkerchiefs
    (d)   Teeth
    (e)   Necks and knees
    (f)   Fingers, hands, nails, etc.

Encouragement and reward should be given. Examples of the desirable should be chosen and exhibited. Please do not exhibit the poorer examples: everyone knows what is bad.'

E

'The appearance of teachers can do a great amount in the "lifting" of the general standard of appearance of the children.'
'It is an obligation of teachers that they insist at all times on the highest forms of behaviour, both in the classroom and the playground. Boys should be encouraged to "Raise Caps".'

The teacher is expected to be minutely attentive to jobs such as marking the register, correctly handling and calculating such classroom finances as dinner money, and establishing 'foolproof systems of distributing and collecting books'. He is urged to have 'clear-cut ideas' about the work in hand:

'We are emerging from the Era of Flabbiness in which hard work was regarded as an evil from which children were at all costs to be preserved. The basic facts of calculation, the mechanics of writing English, the factual backgrounds of history, geography and science, and other sound learning—ALL THESE THINGS CAN BE ACQUIRED ONLY BY MENTAL EFFORT ON THE PART OF THE LEARNER.
Some of the effort may be enjoyable, but some of it must be drudgery, and we shall be deceiving ourselves, and depriving our pupils of their birth-right if we pretend that our schools can be run without a great deal of sheer hard work on the part of ALL concerned.'
'When you have completed a stage in factual teaching of any subject, find out by testing, how much has been retained by the class. If you don't, how do you know whether you have taught the thing at all?
Let your pupils know the results of your tests. Decorate your classroom walls with place lists, with merit lists and progress graphs.'

These introductory notes set out the rules about corporal punishment (only by the Headmaster, in the presence of a witness), the details of the House system, the Prefect system, the school uniform, regular examinations, and the courteous reception of visitors—

'Visitors of the VIP type will be greeted by classes standing.'
The notes end with a prayer:

'Help me to build a child whose wishbone will not be where his backbone should be; a child who will know Thee—and that to know himself is the foundation stone of knowledge.
Lead him, I pray, not in the path of ease and comfort, but under

the stress and care of difficulties and challenge. Here let him learn to stand up in a storm; here let him learn compassion for those who fail.'

It was an integral part of Mr. River's view of education that his school should be streamed—'A', 'B', and 'C'—from the age of seven. It is so integral that he finds it difficult to discuss streaming without drawing in other sides of school life.

'You've got to have streaming. I'm a realist and children are realists. In this school we don't tolerate mediocrity. Everyone has to give of his best, and you get the best out of children by competition. Here we have fourfold competition; competition in class, competition between classes, competition between houses, competition between schools.

There are about 24.3 per cent. grammar school places in this district, and it's no coincidence that we get way above that, every year. It's no coincidence that our cricket team is seldom beaten, it's no coincidence that we sometimes can't get teams to play us, it's no coincidence that we've been in the final of the football cup every single year. Now I'm not trying to say how good we are. All I want to point out is that it's no coincidence—it's for a reason. We pull the very best out of our children.

I know there are people against streaming—airy fairy types, like some school managers and local councillors. They talk a lot of glib clap-trap, that doesn't mean anything, about the *life* of the child, and so on. Most of these airy fairies are only interested in education for other reasons. It's fashionable to get up and make a cry about education, but they're not doing it for the good of education.'

Mr. Rivers organizes his streaming in what the national questionnaire revealed to be a very common way. When the children enter from the Infant school at 7, they are accompanied by a recommended 'A', 'B' or 'C' grading. He divides them into three classes according to this grading, and allows them 10 days to settle in. They are then given a Schonell Reading Test and a Moray House Picture Intelligence Test. After studying the results he makes some transfers—

'Anyone with an IQ of 109 I regard as grammar school material, always remembering that 6 points either way is nothing with such a test.'

At the end of their first term he sets them an examination on the work that they've been doing, and again transfers as he sees fit.

'You soon learn to pick out the children who are receptive and amenable to teaching, or in other words the intelligent ones, and there's your "A" stream for you.'

Transfers do continue to take place at the end of the first, second and third year. He expects these to affect about 5 per cent. of the children. Sometimes it may be the same 'borderline' child being moved up and down each time, difficult to settle in the 'A' stream yet obviously 'top' of the 'B' stream—on the brink, yet unable to leap the widening gap.

The staff

Mr. Rivers's staff is loyal, long-serving and hard-working. After a few years under him, most of the men and one or two of the women expect to get a Headship themselves, and over recent years they have been consistently successful in this. He has six men teachers and seven women. They all work long hours and they work as a team. It is one of his rules that they must take tea together in the staffroom, and not busy themselves with isolated tasks in the classroom. And in the staffroom itself it is a daily experience for Mr. Rivers to stop a teacher plugging away at a pile of mechanical marking, distribute the work round the room and calling out the answers himself, reduce an hour's lonely work to ten co-operative minutes. The atmosphere is almost always cheerful, buoyant with obvious, tangible success.

I can best present this staff by confining my attention to the three teachers who take the last year group. Mr. Wardle of 4C is a tall, stooping man, given to making droll remarks from a corner of the staffroom. He is the school joker, and in one or two ways set apart from the other men. His union is the NUT (National Union of Teachers), whereas the other men belong to the smaller, one-sex and more militant NAS (National Association of School masters). During school hours he usually wears a white or brown smock to protect his clothes, much as if he were a supervisor in a cabinet works. He is the only member of the staff who objects to streaming which he calls 'cramming not teaching', but he never raises the issue in public. He is kindly and paternalistic with children. When the Head praises his class model of the *Cutty Sark*—as he frequently does—he glows with uncontrollable pride.

Mr. Frond of 4B is always tidily dressed, but in noticeably old clothes. He is frequently splashed with paint or marked with whitewash, and has no hesitation in dirtying his hands by crawling under the hutches to free a trapped hen, or in rolling up his sleeves and helping pupils paint a rabbit hutch. His relationship with the children is very free and easy, a perpetual stream of jokes. The children like him, and pester him a shade too much at break times. If a child came to the staffroom door, it was usually to ask Mr. Frond a question. He talks a lot about his pupils' successes when they exhibit their animals alongside other schools:

'Surely "B" children look after animals best. "C" children aren't capable, and "A" children have too many other interests—but with a "B" child it's just *natural.'*

Streaming he accepts as reasonable and efficient, and has only mild and passing criticism to make, whereas he can list many points in its favour:

'I've got reservations about streaming. If I were Head I'd give them not 10 days, but a term to settle down. Then I'd stream them.'

Mr. Bawden who takes 4A is a small, very smart man, usually dressed in white shirt, club tie and dark suit. He is well on the way to a Headship, and talks readily about teaching problems and methods. He has not taught 'B' or 'C' stream children for some time.

'But I *have* taught the dimwits. In fact when I left college I thought that was what I would do—teach the dimwits. Amazing how dim those dimwits are, but I did quite well, got quite good results. Of course it's a few years since I taught any of them now.'

He has taken his present class for 3 years—ever since they were 8 years old. As in quite a few streamed schools, the 'A' stream teachers pick up a class in their second junior year and keep them until they leave the school at 11. This doesn't happen in the 'B' or 'C' stream.

'I like to get them in their second year when they're really malleable. They come from a woman and it's easy—you just work them till they almost drop: basic stuff. You can push the boys a long way, not quite as far with girls—they kick back quicker. Then the second year you only have to cruise along. Work becomes a habit, and they get used to the idea that less than 80 per cent. is a failure mark. It's all over, really, by the third year when the exam comes up.'

His 11-plus results have been outstanding. In a class of 40, 34 will go to grammar school. A further 4 won the necessary marks, but not the necessary recommendation from the school that is asked for with 'borderline' results. The staff did not think that these four would be successful at grammar school largely because of their home backgrounds. One girl out of the 'B' form will also go to grammar school. She had arrived at Honey Bell just prior to the 11-plus examination and had had to be put in the 'B' class because of space shortage.

Mr. Bawden seems curious about what will happen to the pupils when they leave him for the grammar school, but he has no information on this:

'Look at that lad with the brown jumper. I've got him through, but will he last there? But it's not my fault if they're not kept up to scratch by the next teacher.

Every year till this the parents came up and asked whether I could get their kid to grammar school. This year I've done it—but they still come up! They want to know whether their kids will get on OK at grammar school. Well, what more do they want! Talk about a socialistic society! I've done my job, someone else can look after them now.'

With children he is aloof and imperious, very much the schoolmaster. Only the Head is held in more awe by them, and Mr. Bawden's reputation in the neighbourhood is titanic.

The children

In order to discover how the school affected the children I decided to compare the first junior year (7 year olds) with the last junior year (11 year olds). I looked first at academic standards. From the school records[1] I could see that both groups

---

[1] School records are of course only a rough guide. I have no means of knowing how correctly tests were administered or recorded.

had entered the junior school reasonably well grounded in reading. At the age of 7, about 45 per cent. left the Infant School each year with a reading age of *more* than 7 years, and about 25 per cent. were promoted with a reading age of 6 or under. There was no absolute non-reader in either year. This is certainly a very good base for a junior school. Within these scores lay a very wide spread, since a few pupils came to school at five already reading, whereas others had never possessed a book of their own. There were four children with reading ages four years in advance of their age (i.e. 11 plus), so that at seven, before streaming began, a gap of up to 6 reading years had already opened between the extreme children. The child's stream at 7 largely matched his reading ability. The average reading age of 7 year old children just entering the 'A' stream was 8.2 years, for the 'B' stream it was 6.6 years, and for the 'C' stream 5.5 years. Thereafter it was possible to follow progress up the school.

TABLE 19

Chronological Age	Average Reading Age		
	'A' stream	'B' stream	'C' stream
7	8.2 yrs.	6.6 yrs.	5.5 yrs.
8	11.5 yrs.	8.9 yrs.	7.4 yrs.
9	12.7 yrs.	9.8 yrs.	8.1 yrs.
10	13.6 yrs.	11.0 yrs.	9.4 yrs.

These are very good scores. But leaving aside the generally high attainment, we can see that the attainment levels move on as three distinct blocks. The 'B's never catch up with the 'A's, and the gaps between them widen. The slight coming together at the 10 year level is caused by the nature of the tests (whose maximum score is 14 years, as many 'A' children are underestimated).

I was myself able to confirm the validity of the school records, by giving the Schonell Eentence Reading Test, an NFER Mechanical Arithmetic Test, and the Moray House Picture Intelligence Test to all children in the fourth year. On such standard tests we would expect the average score to be around the 100 mark. The results were as follows:

TABLE 20
AVERAGE SCORE: 103—11 YEAR OLD CHILDREN

	'A' stream	*'B' stream*	*'C' stream*
Arithmetic	129	105	94
Intelligence	122	108	99
Reading	118	104	93

No mean performance.

Social class and birthday

How did this impressive academic standard relate to the selection process, by social background and date of birth, analysed in Chapter 2? The 7 year olds were divided socially as follows:

TABLE 21
SOCIAL CLASS OF 105 7-YEAR OLD CHILDREN

Fathers' occupation	*'A' stream*	*'B' stream*	*'C' stream*
Professional and Managerial	22%	9%	9%
Clerical	40%	31%	24%
Skilled Manual	32%	43%	57%
Semi-skilled Manual	6%	17%	10%
Unskilled Manual	0%	0%	0%
Total	100%	100%	100%

Here is much the same process of social class into school class illustrated in Chapter 2. But the community is exceptional in two respects. Firstly, there is a rather higher than usual proportion of middle-class citizens. Secondly, there are no unskilled workers in this table at all. This is the result of the new town's demand for high-grade skills. It may possibly help a little in explaining the above-average academic standards of the school. Presumably in a different environment some of these 'C' children would have been educated as 'B' children, in a different mesh of school expectations.

The sample of 11 year olds here did contain an unskilled workers' group (sometimes labourers who had helped with the early construction of the new town), but again there was rather more than the national average of middle-class children distributed in the customary way between 'A', 'B' and 'C' streams:

TABLE 22
SOCIAL CLASS OF 103 11-YEAR OLD CHILDREN

Father's occupation	'A' stream	'B' stream	'C' stream
Professional and Managerial	20%	10%	7%
Clerical	41%	40%	28%
Skilled Manual	33%	25%	35%
Semi-skilled Manual	3%	15%	17%
Unskilled Manual	3%	10%	13%
Total	100%	100%	100%

On the other hand the effects of birthday were not very marked at Honey Bell. There was an extremely slight difference in the first year—the average age of the 'A' class being 7 years 2.6 months, of the 'B' class 7 years 2.4 months and of the 'C' class 7 years 2.1 months. In the fourth year this had widened somewhat. At the end of the junior course the 'A' stream's average age was 11 years 3.9 months, the 'B' stream 11 years 2.9 months, and the 'C' stream 11 years 1.3 months. Uneven entry into the infant school was not having much effect on Honey Bell. But against that, it was an advantage to be an older child *within* a year group—older children tending to be promoted up the streams and younger ones demoted, until a barely perceptible difference widened into a distinct crack.

Transfer from stream to stream

Mr. Rivers was quite adamant that each child who deserved transfer from one stream to another, received it. In this he was much like every other Headmaster I talked to. But in practice

61

how many earned a transfer? It was possible to look back over the careers of the 11 year old children. When these pupils entered the school they each carried an Infant school recommendation of 'A', 'B', or 'C'. After they had been tested as previously described, they were streamed. The junior school Head agreed with the Infant School recommendation in 85 per cent. of the instances, and disagreed in 15 per cent. At the end of the first junior school year there was a transfer of 7.6 per cent.; at the end of the second and third years, one of 4.2 per cent. each time.[1] These transfers tended to confirm further the Infant recommendation and to widen the age gap a little. The main difference was that the Infant Head seems to have overrated girls and underrated boys, so that on the whole boys were promoted up-stream in the junior school. The one 11-plus success that she didn't forecast was a boy. Yet even so, the 'A' stream at 11 is still distinctly dominated by girls, whereas the 'C' stream is very much a boys' class.

Free transfer from stream to stream is Mr. Rivers's aim. From a study of the academic records we can see that there is an increasing gap between each stream. There are children whose standard attainment seems to merit a transfer. But despite paper qualification and the Headmaster's approval, transfer remains quite a small matter—and children often refuse to settle in a new stream. Partly this is because you cannot move one child up unless you move another child down. But partly it is restricted by teachers' opinions of children's capabilities, and partly too by the children's picture of themselves in relation to others.

Whatever the reasons, free transfer is accepted as an ideal, yet both in this and in other streamed schools I visited, the ideal flow is reduced to a mere trickle, and the original placing in streams is more often final than not. Thirty-three per cent. of the fourth year age group had been selected for grammar school. *With only one exception,* all these children were picked out as grammar school prospects by their Infant Head by their seventh birthday. The problem is to know whether this is a

---

[1] Daniels, J. C. in the *Brit. J. Educ. Pysch.*, February 1961, quotes transfer figures of 6.78 per cent. (first year), 5.67 per cent. (second year), 5.67 per cent. (third year) on a sample of 27 streamed schools that he studied.

shrewd and accurate analysis of different types of children, or whether it is the internal logic of the 'self-fulfilling prophecy'.

The children who lead

I looked next at the children who held any prominent position in school life. To be a member of one of the school's very successful sport teams was a matter of considerable importance. The football team had lost only one match during the season, and the netball team none. I watched both teams in action, and it was immediately clear why they were so successful. It wasn't just their skill which earned victory, though they had that. The Honey Bell children were much fiercer, more determined and resilient. Their tackling was harder, their will to win intense and steadfast, their refusal to accept setbacks, constant. On the field they shouted encouragement or orders to each other; on the touchline their teachers roared permanent support. They cared deeply about taking a further two points in the League Table or knocking another team out of the Cup. If they were beating a smaller school 30-0 at netball, they still treated their opponents with complete seriousness, and went all out to make it 31-0. They certainly met teams of their own kind, but some of the schools they encountered hadn't managed to put their sport on this plane, and a match with them made the Honey Bell players look strangely adult and professional in the art of winning. I noticed that the local Vicar often watched the Honey Bell football team: in conversation he had little to say about the skills they displayed, but was full of admiration for what he called 'character in action'.

In school much was made of victory in sport. Cups and shields were prominently displayed, there were speeches and clapping in Assembly. So far as I could judge the whole school identified itself with the teams, and each stream contributed some players. It was accepted that the lion's share went to the 'A' stream, and that the Captains were 'A' children, but otherwise everyone else was in on the show. Thus both cricket and football captains were 'A' stream boys, 3 of the players came from the 'C' stream, 8 from the 'B' and 11 from the 'A'. Since more girls than boys got into the 'A' stream, their dominance in sports such as netball was much more marked.

A second type of prominence in school belonged to Prefects and House Captains. Again, a great deal was made of these offices, there was a certain amount of public ceremony and special rights. Both the Head Boy and the Head Girl were 'A' stream children, as were all five Prefects. Three of the four House Captains were 'A' children, and one was a 'B'. Exactly the same was true of the Deputy House Captains. No child held more than one of these positions, so that they were shared around. No 'C' stream child qualified for office, and in so far as I knew the school, I could not see any 'C' stream pupil who had the qualities that were expected, and yet was overlooked. I had no means of knowing whether this meant that only 'A' children had the Prefectorial attributes (identification with the teacher, pleasure in, and ability to use command, delight in the special rights, badges, or deference that the office gave). On the other hand it could mean that the 'B' and 'C' children had adjusted to all this long ago, and had necessarily built up different behaviour patterns, or entered the school with them.

Through the children's eyes

How did all this look through the children's eyes? I tried talking about the matter with children, and thought of persuading them to write short passages on it. But I had to abandon this, partly because of the school's attitude (I was already taking up a great deal of time) and partly because the children couldn't think about streaming in isolation.[1] To them it seemed indistinguishable from the nature of existence. One afternoon, when I felt I could not take the school's time up much longer, I asked all the First year and all the last year children to answer these three questions. I was casting round for last minute clues.

[1] In a survey reported by the West Riding Education Authority (July, 1962), 160 older children in 'C', 'D' or 'E' streams of secondary modern wrote on 'What I like and do not like about being in a 'C' or 'D' stream'. 19 mentioned neglect ('I don't like Holy Joe because wenever we come into is room he treats us like convicts he says we ort neverto be in this school'), 19 mentioned inferiority ('Practicly everybody treats you like a scruff'), 14 mentioned your prospects of a job ('If you tell outsiders that you are in a d form they think we are not very clean . . .'), and 15 complained of lack of responsibility. Against this 49 liked being with their form friends, 39 said the work was easier, and 21 mentioned the personal attention they received.

TABLE 23

11 YEAR OLD 'A' STREAM CHILDREN—
THE FAMOUS PERSON I WOULD LIKE TO BE:
74 CHOICES BY 37 CHILDREN.

School	Pop Singers	Films and TV	Sport	'Figures of State'	Others
Sir Edmund Hillary 6	Connie Francis 9	Marilyn Monroe 2	Pat Smythe 2	Queen Elizabeth 1	My Teacher 1
Dr. Albert Schweitzer 5	Cliff Richard 4	Diana Dors 2	Bobby Smith 1	Field Marshal Mont- gomery 1	Class- mates 8
Sir Winston Churchill 2	Adam Faith 3	Jayne Mansfield 2	Johnny Haynes 1	Bessie Braddock 1	
Group Captain Bader 2	Elvis Presley 2	'Guy Gibson' 2	Jimmy Greaves 1		
John Wesley 3	Frankie Vaughan 1	Bruce Forsythe 1	Danny Blanch- flower 1		
Shakes- peare 1		Dale Robert- son 1	Anita Lons- borough 1		
Nelson 1					
Captain Scott 1		Rowdy Yates 1			
Elizabeth Fry 1		Will Hutchins 1			
Lord Shaftesbury 1		Gracie Fields 1			
23	19	13	7	3	9

1. *If you weren't yourself, which famous person would you like to be? You can choose two if you wish.*

2. *Who, in your honest opinion, is the most handsome boy in your year? ('A', 'B' or 'C' class)*

3. *Who, in your honest opinion, is the most beautiful girl in your year ('A', 'B' or 'C' class)*

Of course none of these questions is likely to produce crisp truths about streaming: but as a dipstick into the child's world, the results seemed worth recording.

I was unable to derive any clear pattern from the way 7 year old children answered the first question. The differences from stream to stream were negligible. The most popular choices were the people after whom the Houses were named—Sir Winston Churchill, Sir Edmund Hillary, Group Captain Douglas Bader, Dr. Albert Schweitzer; then came a group of types (ballet dancer, teacher, nurse, film star); a collection of people they had heard about in lessons—Robingsise Grouse, Selanslt (Sir Lancelot) etc. There was also a small group of popular singers, sportsmen, and 'my dad'.

But this altered by the time the children were 11 and had been streamed for 4 years. The choices of the 'A' stream children are shown on page 65.

The first column lists people whom they may have heard about in lessons or through the school House system. The second and third distinguish between two parts of the mass media, and the others are self-explanatory. Commentary on these answers must be highly speculative, but the individual answers may reveal something of the world through children's eyes. For the 'A' child, the most prominent of these groups was the 'school'; whereas for the 'B' children 'school' and popular singers changed places (see table on page 67).

With the 'C' children, the balance swung completely the other way. School figures were negligible, and almost every child in the class desired to be a popular singer. Figures of state are noticeably prominent, as if the 'C' children are only too delighted to be part of the admiring crowd when the Queen, or Mr. Macmillan, or President Kennedy go by. Sport, far from being anti-academic, was associated with the 'A' class—as was noted before in the discussion of teams. My request was mis-

TABLE 24

11 YEAR OLD 'B' STREAM CHILDREN—

THE FAMOUS PERSON I WOULD LIKE TO BE:

57 CHOICES BY 29 CHILDREN.

School	Pop Singers	Films and TV	Sport	'Figures of State'	Others
Sir Winston Churchill 4	Cliff Richard 9	Diana Dors 2	Floyd Patter- son 1	The Queen 2	A million- aire 1
Sir Edmund Hillary 1	Adam Faith 3	Marilyn Monroe 2	Herb Elliot 1	Princess Margaret 1	Class- mates 2
Robinson Crusoe 3	Shirley Bassey 3	Rock Hudson 2	A champion swimmer 1	Princess Anne 1	
Sir Francis Drake 2	Helen Shapiro 2	Bruce Forsyth 1			
Nelson 2	Alma Cogan 2				
Bonnie Prince Charlie 1	Connie Francis 2				
Richard I 1	Joan Regan 1				
Napoleon 1					
Swiss Family Robinson 1	Lonnie Don- negan 1				
Florence Nightingale 1					
17	23	7	3	4	3

understood, and each 'C' stream child gave back three choices, not two (see Table 25).

Honey Bell

TABLE 25

11 YEAR OLD 'C' STREAM CHILDREN—THE FAMOUS PERSON I WOULD
LIKE TO BE: 74 CHOICES BY 25 CHILDREN.

School	Pop Singers	Films and TV	Sport	'Figures of State'	Others
Group Captain Bader 2	Tommy Steele 10	Diana Dors 2	Bobby Charlton 1	Mr. Mac-millan 4	
	Cliff Richards 9	Jayne Mans-field 2	Pat Moss 1	President Kennedy 2	
Sir Winston Churchill 1	Russ Conway 7				
	Adam Faith 2	Marilyn Monroe 2		The Queen 2	
Sir Edmund Hillary 1	Lonnie Don-negan 2	Marty Wilde 2		King George VI 2	
	Alma Cogan 1	Bruce Forsythe 2		Duke of Edin-burgh 1	
	Elvis Presley 1	Petula Clark 2		Princess Anne 1	
	Billy Fury 1	Eamonn Andrews 2		Princess Margaret 1	
	Frank Sinatra 1	Sabrina 1		Lord Baden Powell 1	
	Matt Monroe 1	Maurice Chevalier 1			
	Rose-mary Squires 1	Annette Page 1			
		Margot Fonteyn 1			
4	36	18	2	14	0

Besides the value of individual answers, there may be some kind of pattern emerging here, and it can be seen if we simplify the groups into three:

Stream	School Figures	Mass Media	Others
'A'	34%	41%	25%
'B'	19%	54%	27%
'C'	6%	70%	24%

The streaming in school life interlocks with a streaming in adult life. On the divisions present in the school, the mass media build an audience. It is as if we are on the brink of tracing some links between the great triads of British social life—'A', 'B' and 'C' stream; grammar school, technical and secondary modern; Third programme, Home Service and Light; Upper class, middle class, working class; men of gold, silver and bronze. The links between working class life, the 'C' stream, secondary modern school, and commercial TV seem to be real enough. If this were valid, the question that it poses is: does education necessarily follow cultural difference and cultural poverty in society, or does it not only follow, but institutionalize it—mildly steering the child into the appropriate position for the mass media to take over?

The final two questions put to the children ('Who is the most handsome boy and beautiful girl?'), were a last, oblique attempt to catch a little of the child's point of view. The 7 year old children made their choices as follows:

TABLE 26

THE BEST-LOOKING 7 YEAR OLD CHILDREN

	A child in the 'A' stream	A child in the 'B' stream	A child in the 'C' stream
'A' stream children chose	85%	9%	6%
'B' stream children chose	26%	70%	4%
'C' stream children chose	5%	38%	57%

F

The great majority of 'A' stream children thought that the most beautiful girl or handsome boy was in their own stream, but 9 per cent. made a 'B' stream choice, and 6 per cent. a 'C' stream. The bulk of the 'B' and 'C' stream also chose a classmate, but there was a strong tendency to see beauty residing in the next stream above. To my own judgement outstanding beauty was distributed at random between all streams in all years.

The answers given by 11 year old children were noticeably different.

TABLE 27

THE BEST-LOOKING 11 YEAR OLD CHILDREN

	A child in the 'A' stream	A child in the 'B' stream	A child in the 'C' stream
'A' stream children chose	98%	2%	0%
'B' stream children chose	30%	70%	0%
'C' stream children chose	7%	3%	90%

After four years in their class, the 'A' stream is confident that it contains the beautiful children. The 'B' stream is split between class loyalty and 'A' stream beauty. The 'C' stream has retired in on itself, and is fairly certain that its looks are good looks. No 'A' or 'B' stream child agrees. Beauty itself is streamed.

Summary

Honey Bell school is physically superb. Built in one of England's new towns, it represents a new start in life for families whose own education chiefly took place in old cramped buildings elsewhere. It has a capable and energetic Head, a loyal and stable staff. Formal academic standards are high, and a very wide spread of attainment crystallizes into three distinct blocks. Each stream is encouraged to develop a special set of skills, and in their different ways the animal care of the 'B' stream, and the wookwork of the 'C' stream are as outstanding as the academic excellence of the 'A's. There is a virile interest in competitive sport, and a Christian basis to school life. The needs of each child, whatever his stream, are considered by the staff, and there is far less coarse comment on below-average children than I heard in many other streamed schools. Each town or city has primary schools which are something of a showpiece, and Honey Bell has a little of this status.

The school is organised in the traditional spirit that is common to most primary schools. As we have seen, this means that a process of selection by social class and even by date of birth, is taking place. It means too that the school accepts that for practical purposes there are roughly three types of children with distinct but different skills. This is not hidden at all, and I never had any difficulty in recognizing which were 'C' classes and which were 'A'; and sometimes I had no difficulty in spotting which were 'A' teachers and which were 'C'. The twin principles of selection and competition were visible at work everywhere.

The children saw them too. In the staff's view the children were 'realists' and accepted the broad differences reflected by streaming. The questions I put to the pupils confirmed this recognition. I would not put any great weight on the answers, but record them since they suggest the inarticulate case that the children cannot themselves put. The answers imply that the streaming process controls friendships and tightens the groups further, and that some children, accepting the ABC hierarchy, aspire to worlds above them, locating good looks and ideal friends there. They also suggest the way in which streaming endorses the mesh of parents' education, social class and friendship, and relate this to the mass media and to leadership or establishment images in society. Where schools leave off, the entertainment and advertising world may take over.

I do not know how typical Honey Bell school is. In its streaming process and attitude to children it is, I believe, fairly characteristic. It represents a goal at which other schools aim. In the buildings and equipment with which it is endowed, it is, of course, unusual. Also in the low number of unskilled workers' children attending it. I studied it because a picture of its detailed life and feeling gave me some sense of what lay behind the general sample of streamed schools reported in Chapter Two. But one further patch of detail is missing before any overall picture can be found. The next chapter considers what the Honey Bell parents thought of their school, of the purpose of education and the universal process of early selection through the 11-plus examination and primary school streaming. How much did the school begin all this, how much did it take up and crystallize looser but existing differences and values?

5

WHAT THE PARENTS SAID

THE children lived in the gay and spacious modern houses surrounding the school, whose contrasts of brick and wood boarding created such an air of festival when the sun shone, and the terraces, crescents, avenues and squares hummed with boys and girls. Elsewhere only the wealthier middle class could hope to live in houses so roomy, bright and seriously designed. Pride in the new houses was everywhere felt in the enchanting variety of open gardens: vines climbing up a wall, curling hedgerows made of tall golden-yellow chrysanthemums, clumps of feathery pampas grass ten foot high, and roses spilling petals on the unfenced lawns. Of course there were complaints; of inadequate privacy, transport, amenities built in the wrong order. There was suspicion of modern design 'the wood harbours insects', 'bound to make the house cold, those metal window frames'. There was regret for odd details of the past, discarded by the architects—'which is the front door and which is the back, tell me that.' 'I *do* miss the sound of the gate creaking. I miss that more than anything, a gate clicking and creaking.' But by any standard, the children were growing up in excellent physical surroundings; damp, grime, overcrowding, or the lack of hot water, bathrooms and lavatories were unknown to them.

Inside, the homes were colourful and comfortable. Walls were painted in modern pastel shades; furniture was more old-fashioned; plump, cushioned and deep, seldom angular, metallic and Scandinavian. New TV sets were universal and washing machines and fridges plentiful: every shop in town sported large HP advertisements, and salesmen earned easy livings talking over housewives on the doorstep. Husbands had done their share in building up the home: every man a handyman. A common improvement was folding breakfast bars in the larger kitchens, but often enough the man had done something more adventurous than he would have dared in Islington or Bethnal Green. Mr. Simmonds had created a dining area by dividing his lounge with a screen of bamboo poles thickly entwined with climbing greenery. Mr. Mitchell had put up a huge 6 foot by 2 foot coloured photo of snowy mountains, pine trees and glimmering lakeside, that began on one wall, crossed a corner and ended on another.

It was a new start in life, completely different from the conditions under which the parents had grown up—'Back home we were sleeping 4 in a room. It was like a jigsaw puzzle getting in and out of bed.' 'In London, one window gave us a view of a coalyard, another gave us the railway sidings, and another gave us a view of a window opposite having a view at us.' Many of them now had had 8 years of the new life. They have plenty of grumbles and an increased sense of what you *can* grumble about in life: they have learned how much of man's environment can be changed, knocked down, abolished, rebuilt, planned. But all agree that whoever the new town fails, it serves its huge population of children magnificently.

Having become familiar with the school and the children there, I decided that the next step was to visit the parents of the 7 year old children. It proved possible to visit 88 of these homes.[1] I wished to compare these homes with those of the Honey Bell children who had recently heard the results of their 11-plus examination; and who had had *all* their education at this one school. There were 64 such children and 58 of their homes were visited, making a total sample of 146. The interviews began in June before the younger children had entered the streamed school, and before the older ones had left it.

---

[1] There were 100 such children. But of the younger children's parents 8 refused to be interviewed, three I failed to contact and one left the district. Of the older children's parents, a further 3 refused, one I failed to contact, and two moved home. In these 146 homes, the mother only was interviewed on 63 occasions, the father only on 28 occasions and both parents on 55 occasions.

What the Parents Said

Parents' own schooling

Most of these children's parents had left school at 14. The children of those who had been educated beyond 14 were commonly more successful themselves at school.[1]

TABLE 28

Percentage of Parents educated beyond 14

	'A' stream	'B' stream	'C' stream	Number
7 year old children	50%	37%	16%	88
11 year old children	35%	25%	22%	58

The parents remembered school as a place of dark rooms, strict discipline, formal lessons—

'There's no comparison between Honey Bell and the school we went to. Ours was an old tup, an old midden. And the teachers were someone far away—like Gods and Goddesses. But these days you see the teacher in the pub and buy him a drink.'

'In my day when we *saw* a teacher, we'd shiver in our boots. *Them* were teachers. Not like this right soft lot they have nowadays.'

'No playing with coloured blocks at my school. It was up on a high stool straightaway, and out with a slate and on with the job: $1 + 1 = 2, 2 + 2 = 4$.'

But after school they had been either enterprising or fortunate, and the sample was largely one of very skilled manual workers together with a good number of homes in which the father was a draughtsman, research metallurgist, production manager, teacher.

Once again the tendency was for middle class children to be in top streams and working class children to be in lower streams, even though on this sample semi-skilled and unskilled workers were heavily under-represented.

---

[1] With the 7 year old children their stream refers to the stream in which they were placed during their first year at the junior school. The difference between parents of 7 and 11 year old children partly turns on the new towns increasing attraction to better trained workers.

TABLE 29
FATHER'S OCCUPATION: 88 SEVEN YEAR OLD CHILDREN

Father's Occupation	'A' stream	'B' stream	'C' stream	Total
Professional and Managerial	7	3	2	12
Clerical	13	11	5	29
Skilled Manual	10	15	12	37
Semi-skilled Manual	2	6	2	10
Unskilled Manual	0	0	0	0
Total Number	32	35	21	88

TABLE 30
FATHER'S OCCUPATION: 58 ELEVEN YEAR OLD CHILDREN

Father's Occupation	'A' stream	'B' stream	'C' stream	Total
Professional and Managerial	5	2	0	7
Clerical	11	8	4	23
Skilled Manual	9	5	4	18
Semi-skilled Manual	1	1	1	3
Unskilled Manual	1	4	2	7
Total Number	27	20	11	58

The professional class on the sample largely came from middle class backgrounds themselves. The managers were more likely to come of upper working class parents, and to have climbed to their present position through determined opportunism. Mr. Smart said:

'I left the old technical school at 15, and worked as a die caster until I cracked up—ill—8 years ago. Someone suggested that when I got better I should have a shot at a trainee managers' course for this laundry company. Me and the wife had a conference, and we decided to start at the bottom all over again. She went out to work, I went on the course at lousy wages—and I've never looked back since. As I said, I was appointed Group Manager last month.'

A good many of the highly skilled workers felt that they'd had two big chances in life to go ahead. The first was service in the Army during the 1939-45 war: this had accustomed them to responsibility or turned an unskilled man into an expert craftsman. The second was the move to the new town. Mrs. Alison recalled:

'Me and the husband left school at 14. It was straight into service for me, laying tables, cleaning silver, lighting fires—6.30 in the early morning to 10 at night, with 2 hours off a day, Thursday afternoon free and every other Sunday afternoon off. Three and sixpence a week I got for that. Kept up till two in the morning when there was a bridge party, and then crying myself to sleep in a little room at the top of the house. You can stick your ladies' houses.

Frank was in the sheet metal. No trade, no nothing. But then along came the war, and he picked up a trade—and then the chance to come here. Now he's Senior section leader in the engineering department—top of the tree!'

The homes were lively, a mixture of the industrial middle class and the new working class. There was pride in house and job, an abundance of household goods and heavy Hire Purchase debts. Buying had become a dominating source of pleasure. Four out of every ten wives worked themselves, and though there was some talk of 'C' stream pupils being 'latch key children', 'lost, with no one at home and a frightened look in their eyes', working mothers were to be found equally in every class. It was the new life that Bermondsey, Stepney, Walthamstow, Cardiff, St. Helens, had never offered them. There was regret for the past and for loss of family connections, but for their children almost everyone preferred the new town. It is not surprising that they expected so much of Honey Bell school.

Seven year old children, background and stream
I shall first consider the 88 children just about to enter the junior school and be streamed as 'A', 'B' or 'C'. I shall consider only some of the environmental advantages or disadvantages

77

TABLE 31

BACKGROUND OF 31 'A' STREAM CHILDREN AT 7 YEARS*

Child's name	Parents middle class	Born in first six months of school year	Father left school 14+	Mother left school 14+	Only child or only one sibling	Could read own name at 5	Parents expect child to leave 17+	Parents know what streaming is
Anne	Yes		Yes	Yes	Yes		Yes	Yes
Anita	Yes	Yes	Yes				Yes	
Andrew	Yes	Yes				Yes	Yes	Yes
Brian	Yes	Yes		Yes	Yes		Yes	Yes
Bridget	Yes	Yes	Yes	Yes	Yes	Yes	Yes	Yes
Beverley			Yes	Yes		Yes		Yes
Clare	Yes	Yes	Yes	Yes	Yes		Yes	Yes
Christopher	Yes				Yes		Yes	Yes
Daryll	Yes		Yes	Yes	Yes		Yes	Yes
Doreen	Yes		Yes	Yes	Yes	Yes		Yes
Dawn					Yes	Yes	Yes	
Gale	Yes				Yes	Yes		Yes
Hillary	Yes	Yes	Yes	Yes	Yes	Yes		Yes
Ian						Yes		Yes
Irene			Yes		Yes	Yes	Yes	
John						Yes	Yes	

BACKGROUND OF 31 'A' STREAM CHILDREN AT 7 YEARS*—(Table 31 continued)

Child's name	Parents middle class	Born in first six months of school year	Father left school 14+	Mother left school 14+	Only child or only one sibling	Could read own name at 5	Parents expect child to leave 17+	Parents know what streaming is
Michael		Yes			Yes		Yes	Yes
Marylin			Yes		Yes			Yes
Merril	Yes	Yes	Yes					Yes
Pearl	Yes	Yes	Yes	Yes			Yes	Yes
Queenie		Yes				Yes	Yes	
Rachel		Yes	Yes	Yes	Yes	Yes	Yes	
Robert		Yes	Yes	Yes	Yes		Yes	Yes
Simon		Yes	Yes	Yes		Yes	Yes	Yes
Sonnie	Yes	Yes	Yes	Yes	Yes		Yes	
Tim	Yes		Yes	Yes	Yes			Yes
Teresa	Yes	Yes	Yes		Yes			Yes
Victor	Yes	Yes			Yes		Yes	Yes
Veronica	Yes			Yes		Yes		
William				Yes	Yes	Yes	Yes	
Yvonne	Yes						Yes	Yes

*In this, and the next background chart, the 'scoring' refers only to the first six columns.

79

TABLE 32
BACKGROUND OF 21 'C' STREAM CHILDREN AT 7 YEARS

Child's name	Parents middle class	Born in first six months of school year	Father left school after 14	Mother left school after 14	Only child or only one sibling	Could read own name at 5	Parents expect child to leave 17+	Parents know what streaming is
Allan		Yes				Yes	Yes	Yes
Albert			Yes		Yes			Yes
Avis								Yes
Brian	Yes	Yes			Yes			Yes
Coral								Yes
Christopher	Yes	Yes		Yes				Yes
Cheryl		Yes				Yes		
Dolores		Yes		Yes			Yes	
Daphne	Yes	Yes		Yes	Yes			Yes
Frank								Yes
John		Yes		Yes				
Jim		Yes		Yes				Yes
Maureen	Yes							
Peter		Yes						Yes
Patricia	Yes							Yes
Prunella								
Ronald					Yes		Yes	
Richard	Yes	Yes						Yes
Rory	Yes	Yes						
Steven		Yes			Yes			
Victor			Yes					Yes

under which they were growing up.[1] The following chart compares the children who were graded as 'C' with those who were graded as 'A'. It lists possible advantages with which the child began school—father in a middle class occupation, being born in the first half of the school year, parents who had education beyond 14 years, being an only child or merely having one brother or sister, and being able to read their own name. The first two columns indicate which parents expected their children to be in full time schooling at 17, and which parents understood what 'streams' were.

If as a crude measure we awarded each child an equal 10 points for every 'Yes' in the first six columns, and made no attempt to distinguish between greater, lesser or related advantages, then the future 'A' stream children averaged 32 advantage points each, the future 'C' children scored only 15. This was before the school even saw them. With the great majority of these children the school was confirming in educational terms inequalities which already existed in social (middle class father, etc.) or fortuitous (born in the right half of the year etc.) backgrounds.

Parents of young 'A' stream children

The detailed texture of home life is helpful in showing what these crude measurements of advantage or disadvantage reflected. I want to look at the homes of these young 'A' stream children and then compare them with the background of the young 'C' stream boys and girls. After that I will consider how the picture looks to 'A' stream and 'C' stream parents of eleven year old children : —

The 'A' stream parents possessed books. A teacher's home would have rows of Penguin Classics, and assorted modern novels in paperback—Homer's *Odyssey*, Maupassant *Short Stories*, Apuleius *The Golden Ass*, Dostoievsky, *Crime and Punishment*, C. P. Snow *The Masters*, Kingsley Amis *Lucky Jim*. A civil servant, himself born into a middle class family, might display full sets of Trollope, Dickens, Scott, and buy *The Children's Newspaper* or *The Young Elizabethan* for his son.

---

1 This is not to deny that some of the factors now to be considered may contain an element of innate ability.

What the Parents Said

The home of the skilled workman, or rising works manager, was different. Mr. Martin's shelves contained *The Practice of Management, Modern Engineering Practice,* and a full set of the *Oxford Junior Encyclopaedia.* and the *Book of Knowledge* stacked beneath his TV set. Mrs. Marshall had bought the *Children's Encyclopaedia Brittanica* which stood in a bookcase by itself—expensive, hardly used after the first month, but a visible statement of ambitions and values everywhere present in her conversation about their son, Daryll.

Besides books, there were often adult-approved comics in the 'A' stream homes—*Eagle, Robin. Finding Out About Science.* Besides the ever-present collections of dolls or dinky cars there were also jigsaws, expensive constructional kits, word games on plastic bricks or playing cards. These were toys which required adult guidance or participation, frequently involved the mastery of new logical skills and (even for children still too young to read) the recognition of matching letters or words.

And besides the books and the toys, and the parents who read of an evening, or wrote letters, or took notes, there was conversation. Often the interview in the 'A' stream home was quite distinctive because the parents could relate personal experience to general thoughts on education; they were more at ease in marshalling arguments, spotting logical inconsistencies, moving freely in conceptual language.[1] Theirs was the language of ideas as well as of first hand experience; and language which approximated to prevailing grammatical conventions.

As soon as they could talk, their children began to speak a language which education, or social standing, or self-improvement had given their parents. The children admired and imitated parents who often consulted books or wrote letters. They played games which gave them valuable pre-school experience of logic, numbers, words. They were ready to read by the age of five, and speaking an embryo language which would give them relatively little trouble with problems of grammatical usage or the deployment of rational ideas. At five, ambitions to

[1] See Bernstein, B., 'Social Class and Linguistic Development: A Theory of Social Learning', Halsey, A. H., Floud, J., and Anderson, C. A., *Education, Economy and Society,* for discussion of differences between middle class and working class speech.

read, write and calculate were firmly planted, and many preliminary skills mastered.

Furthermore, certain 'A' stream parents often had a distinctly low view of some of their neighbours:

> 'There's such a lot of low intelligence people in this town. It wasn't like this in Ruislip. All the best people are leaving here. Those that are left talk out loud and go in and out of each other's houses. If you stand at my window you can watch the teapot going round all day on the opposite side of the road.'

> 'I *do* think it would have been better if they hadn't mixed people up so, if they'd *classed* them a bit more. You get it so *slummy* this way.'

Sometimes they had a very keen sense of just being on the 'right' side of the boundary:

> 'Of course, they're not quite the same as us round here. My husband was put on the monthly at the factory. The directors told him he should be eating in the "monthly" canteen now, not the ordinary one ...'

And in everyday life the formal marks of this difference were present in gossip and conversation:

> 'On this road, it's all Christian names. It's all Doll and Pam and Alice, but I can't bring myself to do that—I'm *Mrs.* Emerson.'

> 'I'm determined to stand out against this town, and *they* know it. Oh yes, I hear them calling me nicknames. They call me *Lady* Yorke, or *Duchess* of Yorke, but I don't care. By the time David's got through eleven plus (touch wood), we'll move out and buy a small bungalow.'

In part, streaming at school was defining feelings of 'streaming' in local society, all the more sharply felt because people had not yet sorted themselves out into anything like 'A', 'B' or 'C' neighbourhoods; and working class and middle class, weekly pay packet and monthly cheque, lived side by side.

First months at school

For many of the 'A' stream parents the beginning of school was like the beginning of a race; expectant, excited, they tested their sense of a child's abilities against the reality of school grading. At Honey Bell, the Head of the Infant school recalled that after *a single week* of schooling, one future 'A' parent asked 'how successful is he with his *academic* work, never mind the other', and a second already wanted to know 'Will he pass the 11 plus?'. The Head commented—'We knew Ian would, even then: but of course we couldn't say so'.

The race was on, and the children first sorted themselves out into readers and non-readers. Honey Bell Infants was a relaxed and liberal school. Reading was taught assiduously, but for much of the time the children pursed creative play—building castles, painting lions, singing, listening to stories. The few parents who had had a university education understood and welcomed this: their children were reading anyway, and they were ready to accept that, at this stage (though not later), academic work was one facet of an education which embraced the whole child, often indefinably working through play, drama, music, art.

But the bulk of the 'A' stream parents, who had had a grammar school education and no more, disliked the freedom and the 'play'. Left to themselves they would have demanded a more antique, formal, academic day for their children. As it was, they didn't yet have sufficient familiarity in dealing with the school to be an effective force—if that came, it came later. Many believed that the 'real thing' didn't begin until the junior school anyway: the infant years were almost 'expendible'.

'They're too lax in the Infants. They *lose* six months of real education every year.'

'I'll tell you what's wrong with education. They play about too much in the Infants, they ought to start their education earlier.'

'In the Infants, it's a false paradise. The idea of what work is hasn't sunk in really. When they get into the Juniors, there's spasms and tears because work has got to be done. It's like a slap in the face for them. They should work more in the Infants, and then they wouldn't have trouble in the Juniors.'

The impulse for 'solid', examinable learning—'results'—was coming, not from Honey Bell school alone, but from this group of parents. Of course there was a great deal of sensible and sensitive help:

'As soon as I saw Jean was learning to write italic style, I went to the library and got a couple of books on it.'

'He was learning reading and liking these Noddy books. I found out there were some gramophone records of the stuff, and I bought him them instead of more ABC's—that made a difference, I'm sure.'

—but basically the children were being encouraged to regard markable academic work as being education, and the unmarkable, the imaginative, the time spent on fiction, music, art, as being recreation. On the whole the school accepted and reinforced this.

First impressions of streaming

About a third of all the parents of first year children did not know what streaming was. More 'A' stream parents than 'C' stream parents knew. Many of those who *did* know had had experience of streaming through an older child. At Honey Bell, the Headmaster, Mr. Rivers, took some trouble to explain the system, and regularly outlined it in a little talk on Open Days.

'He was fair and straightforward, and sincere—that's all I can ask for. He said just because a child's in the "A" it doesn't mean he's helped on more than the rest. I mean, I liked his philosophy.'

'It doesn't matter whether a child is in the "A" or the "C"—he looks at them with fatherly pride.'

But some 'A' stream parents had much more rough and ready views than Mr. Rivers:

'You've got to sort them out, and seven's the time to do it. You can spot the nits by then.'

'There's no eyewash about it. If you're not "A" stream material when you come to the Juniors, you're not—and that's that.'

'An "A" stream child ought to be made to feel he's an "A" stream child. He ought to be told that he's different from the others, and that's why he's there. Call it intellectual snobbery if you like, but he's got to have incentive if he's going to get on.'

Like many other Heads, Mr. Rivers had tried using different names instead of 'A', 'B' and 'C', in order to lessen feelings of superiority or inferiority. Some other schools I visited called classes 1 Red, 1 Blue, 1 Green, or 2S, 2J and 2M (using the initial of the teacher). But children and parents soon pierced these thin screens—those who understood what 'A', 'B' and 'C' was all about, understood what Red, Blue and Green concealed.

Mr. Rivers tried dropping 'C' altogether and substituting 'R'—meaning 'Remove'. But parents and children translated this into their own language:

' "A" means grammar school stuff, "R" means "Retarded".'

'The lady next door told me what "R" stood for—"Retarded".'

'Pauline's in a stupor about the "R" class, she says if she goes into that she'll be daft. I keep telling her she's an "A".'

To the parents of the 'A' children, streaming at seven made sense. They were sometimes sorry for children on the other side of the line, but in so far as they understood streaming they believed it reflected the brutal reality of unequal talent that 'B' and 'C' parents must learn to accept.

'Some take it too hard. Take next door—their boy went into the "C" stream. She tackled the wife about it—but there . . . they take it too hard.'

Parents of young 'C' children

The homes of the young children who went into the 'C' stream were usually different. Fewer of their parents had had any secondary education, only occasionally had their schooling been good enough or long enough to develop in them any taste for reading. Their work, with exceptions, demanded no writing from them. Consequently most of the homes had few books (though even here an Encyclopaedia salesman may have sold a little-used set). A copy of the *TV Times* might be the only publication on show: even pens, ink, envelopes, writing paper had frequently 'run out'.

There was conversation: vivid and interesting talk, but it was usually the concrete language of personal experience, of here-and-now, and seldom conceptual, the language of ideas. Nor was its grammar the grammar of the established idiom recognised in schools.

Toys there were in abundance: dolls and dinky cars, seldom the canny or creative toys that linked up so easily with desirable school skills. And parents did hardly any academic teaching in the pre-school period. Sometimes they wanted to, but they knew the technique had changed, and they had no knowledge of the principles.

'We'd like to teach him to say Ay, Bee, Cee, but the way they teach at school now isn't like that. We wanted to help, but we haven't got the style of it, see? So we did nothing.'

'I mean, you don't like to do anything do you. We always talked about "adding up" and "taking away", but Tony says "No, we don't do it that way, we do it *minus*".'

'I'd like to help, but I don't think my word would be worth anything. I don't feel I'm qualified.'

Two of the parents who had an elder child at secondary modern school felt particularly frustrated. They were excited by their children's learning, wanted to join in, but couldn't.

'Ann's very intelligent—she's 13—she's more intelligent than me now. I think sometimes that when the baby's older I might go to night school and catch up with her, and then I'd try and stay with her.'

Sometimes the interviews with 'C' stream parents suggested that a medical analysis[1] might reveal that weaker or distressed children settled in the lowest stream, but I couldn't check this:

'In the Infants she had a respiratory infection and stomach pains. She was 7 weeks off with a cough. I don't think it mattered, because they don't do a lot of work in the Infants, do they?'

'He couldn't go for three months. A milk lorry backed into him and broke his leg. I think they allow for that at school. He should have picked up a bit by now—he has a bit—but I expect he's just lazy. He's in 1C—I think they said it's the bottom—that's where he should be until he starts to work.'

But as the last quotation shows, it was not just a matter of 'C' stream children having had more than their share of ill-health (even if that were true). Their parents, lacking an education themselves, analyzed their child's situation in unhelpful

---

[1] Some evidence is given by Douglas, J. W. B. and Mulligan, D. E., in 'Emotional Adjustment and Educational Achievement' reported in *Proceedings of the Royal Society of Medicine*, Vol. 54, No. 10, October, 1961. Discussing a sample of children with certain nervous symptoms they record that 'At each level of measured ability they are less likely to get a grammar school place than are those with few symptoms, and the extent of their disadvantage may be summarized by saying that they get 10 per cent. fewer places than expected after taking their measured ability into account, whereas the children with few reported symptoms get 2 per cent. more places'. The teachers dealing with these children were not able to perceive this variation, though it concerns children of like ability.

terms—'bone lazy', 'he's 'C' just because he doesn't try', 'happy-go-lucky', 'messes about', 'he hasn't got it, no point in doing much if he hasn't got it'. Mr. Silk's impractical exhortations to his boy, for example, seemed to depress rather than inspire:

'When he comes home I say, "What class are you in, 1C? Well, 1A, that's the class you *ought* to be in." I tell him plain enough.'

But not every 'C' parent had Mr. Silk's clear knowledge of streams.

'Harold's in the "C". I wonder how they select the "C" side?'

'Jim's in "C", but that don't matter. It's what they do at 11 plus that matters, so we're not thinking of Jim much for a few years.'

'Carol is about No. 1. She's in this "C". The lady next door said it's for backward children, but I can't think that's right: she's No. 1.'

'They put him in 1B at first, and now he's changed to 1C. He came home ever so pleased. He must have done well—all his friends are there too.'

Over a third of the 'C' stream parents had no clear idea of what streams were, despite the Headteacher's talks on Open Day. Often (but not always) they were the parents who did not come to Open Days. This was not so much because they didn't care—most parents in the new town certainly cared about education. It was because, having had little education in their own childhood, they felt uncomfortable about presenting themselves at a school, or failed to realise the importance of this personal contact, or were quite unpractised in this kind of social relationship. Sometimes they just did not like competitive education.

It was clear, then, that at Honey Bell streaming at 7 hardened looser groupings already there in society. The children from the higher social class, the small families with some history of education, came to school ripe for reading and number work. The 'A' stream was for them, especially if they had had the fortuitous advantages of health and a strategic birthday. Home began, and school confirmed a network of expectation that encouraged them to set high goals and believe they could achieve them. At the age of 7, three times as many 'A' stream children expected professional jobs (teacher, doctor, etc.) as did 'C' stream children. And their parents' expectations of them were of much the same order.

On the other hand, the 'C' child with a much poorer social and educational background, a larger family and a series of adventitious handicaps was trapped in the net of minimum expectation—however gifted and humane his teachers might be.

Finally, it was noticeable how innocently most parents had moved into the streamed situation, how many—despite the school's frankness—didn't realise what was happening, didn't make direct connections with 11 plus, and the differing futures before the grammar school and the secondary modern pupil. The education system was already steering them along distinctly different courses, and yet so many never knew that—if they wanted them—the moments for decision, discussion and choice were slipping past them.

Streaming at 11 *plus*

The 58 interviews with parents of fourth year children at Honey Bell who knew their 11 plus results clarified this further. For simplicity's sake I shall again contrast 'A' stream and 'C' stream parents.

If we awarded the same crude share of 'advantage points' to this group as we did to the 7 year olds, the 'A' stream children average 32 points, the 'C' stream 14. It is very much like the situation set out in the earlier chart. This time almost all the 'A' stream parents are expecting their child to be in full time education at the age of 17, whereas over a third of the 'C' stream parents still do not understand what streaming is. The familiar pattern of inherited or fortuitous advantage leads to knowledge of the system and high levels of expectation, whereas original or accidental disadvantage encircle the child with minimal ambitions.

'A' stream parents after 11 *plus*

All the 'A' stream parents of these older children knew their child was in the 'A' class; all the 'C' parents knew which class their child was in too. But even at eleven, 3 of the 'B' stream parents thought their child was in the 'A' and 5 didn't know where they were.[1] 'A' parents had doubts about 11 plus, but

1 There is likely, of course, to be a defensive element here.

none about streaming—even if they hadn't liked the idea very much at seven. They praised the Head's candour and realism:

'Mr. Rivers is very, very fair about it. This matter of segregation, the way he does it doesn't embarrass the children at all. Though when he gets the parents at these Open Days, he puts it point blank. He tells them straight—he says if he thinks there's anything in a child at all then, damn it, he'll get it out. And he's got a very good judgement that way, a very good judgement.'

By this age, most of these parents, too, were confident of their judgements of intrinsic ability. A common comparison was:

'It's like eggs—you sort them out, large brains, medium and small.'

And any question of mixing 'A', 'B' and 'C' children was considered with distaste.

'I'm a teacher myself, and I know it's quite impossible to teach older children unless they *are* streamed. I've never been in an unstreamed school, but I imagine it's chaos.'

'I wouldn't like to think of my children being pulled down to the others' level.'

Like the Head of Honey Bell, most 'A' stream parents were interested in results. Numerical statements of their child's progress and ability fascinated them—marks in an exam., IQ scores, percentage of 11 plus passes, number of GCE's at the grammar school last year—these were the stuff of their educational thinking. The Head had sometimes to resist this:

'He told us "under no circumstances can you be told the children's IQs. You can ask the teachers for their reading ages, but they are not allowed to tell you IQs.".'

Nevertheless 'A' stream parents constantly referred to IQs, and commonly quoted figures:

'Reg is about the same as his sister: they're both about 134, so that's not bad.'

Their authority for such statements may have been quite illusory. But the interesting fact was that they came to believe in the IQ figures, it gave them the security of 'results' and confirmed their feeling that the whole 'A', 'B' and 'C' business was about *intrinsic* ability: 'whether a kid's got it or not'.

Eleven plus was now successfully behind them, and (like most of the 'B' and 'C' parents also) they felt it was an indispensable selection procedure. Rather less than a third wanted it adjusted, but none wanted it abolished. They had prepared for it, had expected and encouraged homework, and helped when they could. There were excesses but most parents were caustic over these:

'I thought about getting Eileen a private tutor—my sister did. But really you've got to be pretty dim *not* to get through 11 plus. I mean you *don't* have to carry on like my sister. She kept it up all the time, every hour of the day. I mean, you'd open the lavatory door and there'd be a question in big letters—"What is the name of the Prime Minister?" My sister stuck questions all over the place.'

They were somewhat more worried over the effects of anxiety, bed-wetting, migraine, sickness, that came up from time to time. No parent liked this, or thought it a necessary part of education.

'Allan wet all last summer, and all winter and all this summer. I've been to the doctor's, but he said he couldn't help—just to wait and he'll grow out of it. But Allan worries more when he does it. He doesn't like the little ones to know, but they do know because they go into each other's bedrooms.'

But those whom this did affect saw that it was related to a whole future of advantages, and were prepared to tolerate unpleasant patches now and again in the belief that 11 plus success would amply make up for this.

And when it came, they felt it did. They had a strategic view of the future that few 'C' parents had:

'I always knew myself that she was a grammar school child! I always *knew* it! If we're out for a day and go for a meal, she'll say "Mummy, I can't go into a restaurant in shorts, that's not being properly dressed". And when dad takes us all out for dinner, and asks where shall we go to, she says, "I want to go where lemonade is fifteen shillings a glass". She's always been a grammar school type all right has Clare.'

'C' stream parents after 11 plus

By contrast, even after 11 plus, many 'C' stream parents hadn't clearly realised what had been happening over the last four years. If they knew their son was in a 'C' class, this didn't mean they perceived its nature:

'I don't really understand when they say class this and grade that. I don't follow it. I ought to know. I've been to Open Days and spoken to the teacher, but I don't have the education myself. I can only say they're in the class according to their age.'

'Fay was in the "B" once, but then I found out right by chance from a neighbour that she'd been swopped to the "C". Fay wouldn't tell me. I did speak to the Head, and he explained, but I couldn't see the reasons of it all. Still she's nearly top of her class.'

Realisation that streaming was a mode of preselection from the age of seven came late, if at all:

'We never realised what these "A" and "C" classes were all for until after the 11 plus. It's only since Mike took it that we've cottoned on. You have to learn with your first one, don't you?'

'After Ian coming up the "C" and not getting far, we might get a bit further with young Merle here. I don't know what class they'll put her in, but my opinion—it's only my opinion—is that these "C" classes aren't up to much. They don't get nowhere in them.'

'I've been fostering children for years, and one thing I've noticed. These children never get to the front. Every one of mine has been a "C"; they start in "C" and finish in "C". I don't know what happens, but they never get up.'

Eleven plus had come and gone, and often with a feeling of mild surprise some 'C' parents had discovered that their children were never seriously in the race. They had missed or ignored the crucial moments of selection and decision. If their child was worried and upset, this was in itself sufficient reason for not pressing a course which heightened anxiety: unlike the 'A' parents, they had not the knowledge or experience in this matter to balance present pain against future pleasure, and ignoring the strategies of education, they thought in terms of their child's immediate happiness.

'Lillian didn't want to go in for the exam. It was the time Granny died, and it upset her: it upset us all. So we said, "Never bother, Lil", though afterwards I wish she had.'

It must be stressed again that they were not unhelpful. It was that they were frequently ignorant of the context in which their children were being educated, and such help as they could proffer was emotionally generous but ineffectual:

> 'She needs such a lot of *explaining* done to her. I tell her it's past Mum now! Dad has to take over, but in my opinion it's past him too. I just say to her "Do your best, that's all, nobody can do any better".'

Parents' view of the selection system

In order to clarify how much knowledge of streaming and pre-selection they had, all the parents—both of 7 year old and 11 year old children—were asked a series of general questions. Firstly, they were asked whether an extra term or two in the Infants school mattered; did birthday count for or against a child? About half the parents of the 7 year olds thought it did. Perhaps the closer they were to the original grading into 'A', 'B', 'C', the more aware they were of environmental factors: four years later ideas of innate ability were expected to account for most forms of success or failure at school.

Secondly, parents were asked whether they thought it possible that future grammar school children could mostly be picked out by the age of 7. Only about a third of the parents thought so; a figure that was constant between all streams and at both ages.

Next, they were asked what percentage of children they thought would annually change streams at Honey Bell. The average figure given by the parents of the younger children was 30 per cent., by the parents of the older children, 28 per cent. Only the parents of the older 'A' stream children averaged a rather lower figure—23 per cent. The actual rate of transfer given in Chapter 4 was 7.6 per cent. in the first year, dropping to 4.6 per cent. in later years; a normal figure.[1]

The parents were next asked how many children from 'B' and 'C' streams would normally pass the 11 plus. They were invited to choose either 'none', 'a few' or 'a lot'. The actual

[1] Daniels, J. C. in 'The Effects of Streaming in the Primary School—What Teachers Believe', *Brit. Journ. Educ. Psychol.*, February, 1961, quotes a sample of 173 teachers whose average estimate of transfer across streams was almost 18 per cent. a year.

situation was that normally no such children passed, though exceptional circumstances did occur (e.g. an able child moving into the district immediately before the 11 plus, and having to be seated with the 'B's through lack of space). All the parents were much more optimistic. At seven, only 14 per cent. of the parents expected *no* 'B' child to pass; and 10 per cent. expected 'a lot'. At 11, the idea of 'a lot' of 'B' children passing had disappeared, but even so only 34 per cent. still expected *no* passes. They were more disillusioned about 'C' stream children, but still generous in their estimates. At 7, only 72 per cent. expected *no* passes; a quarter of the parents were expecting 'a few', and 2 of them foresaw 'a lot'. At 11, 76 per cent. had realised there would be no 'C' children going to grammar school, but 17 per cent. were still imagining that 'a few' would. The overestimate was spread widely over all streams, and studying the interviews there seemed to be two definable groups of parents who were considerably optimistic about the chances of lower stream children. The first group was of 'C' stream parents who had not clearly grasped what the 'C' label was all about. The second group were 'A' stream parents who knew perfectly well that their own children would pass, but also imagined that far more children succeeded than in fact did.[1] It was not uncommon for parents to think of 11 plus success, not as being controlled by the number of grammar school desks available in the town, but as simply being the number of children passing an unchanging 'standard' (no doubt they remembered the organisation of their own schooldays). I regretted that I had not asked how many children they thought went to a grammar school anyway, because it was clear that some parents imagined that (in theory at least) *all* the children in a very good year could 'pass'; and I had the impression that the parents here commonly believed that *half* the school population went to grammar schools, though I cannot check this. Certainly their ideas of whether their own child would pass were unrealistic. At seven, 42 per cent. expected their child to succeed (65 per cent. of the 'A' stream, 40 per cent. of the 'B' stream, 11 per cent. of the 'C' stream). This dropped to 31 per cent. (very close

[1] Of course, in this whole range of similar questions there is probably again an element of defensive over- or under-estimate, but I have no means of checking this.

to the actual figure) at eleven years of age. But this last 31 per cent. was not in fact made up of the children who did succeed, for up to the last moment a third of the 'B' parents confidently expected success and odd ones among the 'C' parents too. On the other hand, the 'A' stream parents in their final anxieties underestimated their chances.

Did they then think the 11 plus was a good or bad thing for their children to face? The overwhelming majority believed that success or failure had no connection at all with social class, and well over half thought the system was basically sound, and should be continued exactly as it was. This was true in all streams. About a quarter wanted some changes, and the remainder had no opinions to offer on the subject; they accepted 11 plus without being eager to defend or criticise it. The criticisms offered were extremely mild. A couple of parents wanted less 'secrecy' and said the results (e.g. names, schools and 'marks') should be printed in the evening paper. Half a dozen wanted the Head to have more say, half a dozen wanted him to have none at all. But the remainder developed two points. Firstly, that the assessment be made over a longer period of time—'not just a snap test, but a lot of occasional tests'. Secondly, and if anything this was the really vigorous point of view, many parents wanted not an 11 + but a 12 + or a 13 + :

'It shouldn't be *abolished*, but *altered* in some way. A child develops at different ages. Some develop as late as 12.'

'11 plus is far too early. 12 or 13 is the ideal age, that's when they develop and suddenly grasp things.'

'11 is neither one thing or another. A child grows up at 12.'

Parents' criticism of 11 plus was not at all criticism of selection as such. It was an effort to deal with anxiety, with the observable knowledge that children grew up at a varying pace and that to this the 11 plus chopper was indifferent. There was a popular belief in the existence of some crucial stage of development at 12 or 13.[1] In general the parents discounted environmental factors and thought chiefly in terms of innate ability. If he had 'it', it would come out; if not, then little could be done.

[1] No parent mentioned that selection in the private sector of education takes place at 13 +.

The big difference was that more 'A' parents than 'C' parents began by assuming that their child did in fact 'have it in him'. Their estimates of the flexibility of streaming, ease of transfer and grammar school opportunities for the low-stream child were all exceedingly optimistic. Many wanted the system changed to a more prolonged 12 + or 13 +, sometimes in the belief either that this would increase their own child's chances, or that there was some significant stage of development at these ages. But in no way could the parents be said to be radically critical of the very idea of early selection at 11, and in consequence of pre-selection from 7 years of age.

During the pilot stage of this enquiry I was puzzled by some of this concern to improve only the mechanics of 11 plus selection, and then realised that I had been assuming that parents were aware of alternative modes—especially the comprehensive school. I suppose I thought this because the majority of parents were formerly Londoners, and still retained strong contacts there. Similarly, the majority of them (in all streams) were Labour party voters: supporters of the local government group which had brought comprehensive education to London. But checking this during the main enquiry I see I was quite wrong. Seventy per cent. of the parents did not know what comprehensive schools were. The most knowledgeable were the 'A' parents, of whom half were aware of such schools, but even here it was a somewhat vague knowledge. When the principle of comprehensive schooling was explained to the parents, few disapproved, a third thought it good, and the rest were indifferent. But I doubt if such a polite and unreal exchange, remote from the here-and-now of their child, tells us much of the likely reception for comprehensive schooling in such a district.

Rather more helpful was the fact that nearly two-thirds thought that citizens, through their votes, *could not change* such things as 11 plus procedure. It was hard to define their feeling of remoteness from these matters, but there was a frequent sense of selection being the province of permanent officials in London, or of teachers and administrators beyond the reach of the citizen's vote, who ultimately defined the policies within which the professional educators should work. Only the 'A'

stream parents were somewhat less conscious of being mani-
pulated by a barely challengeable system—and even here more
than half of them thought that citizens did *not* have even remote
control.

As a last stray pointer to the context in which the parents
assessed their child's place and opportunities in education, they
were asked whether private schooling should be abolished, and
all children sent to state schools. Only 13 per cent. thought this
a good idea, and the strongest support of all for private schooling came from 'C' stream parents.

'Public schools are part of the structure of England. You *can't*
get rid of them. Mind you, I think it'd be a good idea if 25 per
cent. of their children came from ordinary schools on a government grant. Sleeping all together in the same building, growing up
together in the same building, it would make them more broad-
minded. Nine out of ten would be leaders—good officer material
and all that.'

'A' stream parent

'They're tip-top these boarding schools. Finest education to be
had. It's regimental, like the Army. It's having a system (like the
Army) that does it. Even the scruffiest recruit is made neat and
trim in no time. That's what you get in public schools, good
discipline.'

'B' stream parent

'I've nothing against them. If I'd thousands to chuck around I'd
send mine there too. It's in us British. I don't begrudge it them. I
don't think a kiddy whose father's got thousands of quid should
have to go to school with a kiddy whose father's got nothing.'

'C' stream parent

Summary

This chapter has tried to illustrate the ways in which a school
such as Honey Bell is reflecting pressures and levels of expectation within a neighbourhood, and the ways in which parents
understand and do not understand its internal processes of
selection. A study of 'A' stream parents showed that their
children began school with a store of family experience, pre-
school skills and fortuitous advantages that connected easily
with 'A' stream status. Existing social differences were translated by the school into new education differences. The 'C'

children came from homes with matching disadvantages, and though the parents cared about education and wished to help their children, their own lack of social and academic skills often meant that their help was generously given but quite ineffective. ('I don't have the education myself'). Their concern with the immediate present of their children's life may have been humanly right, but it made poor educational strategy.

On the whole (and despite the school's efforts), the parents had only a sketchy knowledge of how the selection procedures of 11 plus and streaming were steering their children on differing courses. At 7, a third did not know what streaming was, and this remained true for many lower stream parents at 11. They heavily overestimated transfer between streams and the chances of 'B' and 'C' children making grammar school. They knew little about comprehensive schools, and certainly admired public schools. Their critique of 11 plus could be passionately put, but it was a critique of surface efficiency and not of the thing as such. They were supporters—mildly critical—of the status quo.

Like the teachers, they thought almost always in individual rather than social terms. They ignored the balance of accidental disadvantage, and the different kinds and levels of expectation within which the child's talents were developing, at home and at school.

6

SCHOOLS, STREAMED AND UNSTREAMED

THE children at Honey Bell were streamed. Their gifts developed at different rates and in different directions according to whether they were 'A', 'B' or 'C' children. Behind the streaming technique were teachers' beliefs in types of children and the scarcity of talent; and beyond the teachers were parents endorsing—in a less clear-cut way—feelings about the rarity of excellence, the need to locate it early, and to separate the children of gold from the children of silver and of baser metal.

Before leaving this enquiry I wanted to bring school and classroom back into the foreground again and compare Honey Bell with schools, streamed and unstreamed. I therefore wrote to four local authorities in the North, Midlands and South of England asking for permission to visit a dozen good streamed primary schools, nominated by them. In the event it was possible to collect data from 10 such streamed schools. Since all were chosen by their local authority, we can regard them as being schools in high estimation. Next, ten unstreamed schools were visited, also in the south, midlands and north. The unstreamed schools came from those who answered the questionnaire discussed in chapter two.

Ten streamed schools
The one thing that all 10 streamed schools, chosen by their local authority, had in common was high 11 plus scores. In districts where on average 23 per cent. of the children entered grammar school, this small sample had won 37 per cent. grammar school places in the previous year. Two big schools, each serving middle class suburbs in the north took 50 per cent. each.

Their Heads, like Mr. Rivers at Honey Bell, considered streaming as a form of natural selection: perhaps unfortunate, but unavoidable.

'Most of our children are all right, but over there we draw from a poorer part of the town. The parents are rag sorters in the mills, things like that, so the children are less intelligent, poor heredity, poor environment, poor attitudes—there's nothing you can do about it. They're our "C"s—lucky we don't have many of them.'

This school suffered from lack of space. The 11-year-old 'A's were in a very decent classroom—but there were 47 of them. The 'B's used half of the school canteen as a classroom, and though this was bright and airy, it meant they lost one lesson every day whilst the dinner tables were set up and laid. The rag-sorters' children in the 'C' stream had a class of only 25; but it was held in an old concrete hut at a distance from the main school. Their teacher said:

'This place has been condemned. All day the children have to work with the electric lighting on. And these army coke stoves are no good. Especially since the coke has to be tipped outside and gets soaked in the rain. We have to bring it in, a little pile at a time, and dry it out before we burn it. And this used to be a concrete floor, but the teacher before me developed bad feet, and that made them put the wood down.
It's a pity the children are over here, but it's not altogether a bad thing—they can run around here more, and it doesn't matter much if things get damaged. It might be nice if they mixed in with the rest—the other children might bring their copies of *Knowledge* and things like that. But I'm not sure the others would let them mix—for one thing, this lot smell.'

By contrast 'the others' in the 'A' stream were an enchanting group of children, busy and courteous. Round their walls were pinned neat pages of sums, and a selection of scrupulously accurate paintings. The 'C' children had shouted out answers to their teacher's questions, but these 'A' stream pupils were not easily drawn—and a quiet word or reserved smile often sufficed for an answer.

These characteristics—large, quiet 'A' classes, small but physically separated 'C' classes—repeated themselves in one school after another. In a small mining town the eldest 'C' class shared part of the infant school, a hundred yards from their own buildings. In another northern town they were in a 'prefab' built at the far corner of the school playground. And yet the most gifted teacher seen was taking one of these classes, and the display of imaginative art on her classroom walls went far beyond from any other class, whether 'A', 'B' or 'C'. It was both encouraging and perplexing to encounter this sudden revelation of hidden, non-measurable talent from the children who 'smell'.

It was also unique. On the whole, 'C' classes were not impressive, and the successful and more experienced teachers did not take them, as the following data on their fourth year teachers suggests:

TABLE 33

28 TEACHERS OF 11 YEAR OLD CHILDREN IN 10 STREAMED SCHOOLS

	'A' stream	'B' stream	'C' stream
Average Age of Teacher	44	40	34
Average Number of Years' Teaching Experience	22	16	9
Number holding Graded Posts	8	3	1
Total	10	10	8

Top 'A' stream teachers were older and more experienced, sometimes they were better qualified and usually paid more than their colleagues. In these 10 schools there were 23 'graded' posts. (A graded post brings in a substantial salary increase.) The headteacher decides himself who shall hold such posts in his school, and what duties, if any, they shall perform in return. In these schools the deputy headship (the first 'graded' post) was held in nine out of ten cases by a teacher taking 4A or 3A. Altogether 15 graded posts were held by 'A' teachers, 7 by 'B' teachers and 1 by a 'C' teacher. So these 'A' teachers, by virtue of their longer service, slightly better qualifications, and major share of 'graded' posts drew larger salaries than their 'B' or 'C' colleagues.

This information helped to clear up a problem raised earlier —we can see that children are streamed, and parents are

101

'streamed'; but are teachers 'streamed'? It seems that they some-times are, though some Heads made strong efforts to stop this. When Mr. Hazlehead became Headmaster he recalled that:

'The "A" children ran everything, they got the best equipment and the new books, whilst the rest got the cast-offs. Why! the teachers even called themselves "A", "B" and "C" teachers. I waited a bit and then decided to make a change somewhere. I picked on the woman who had had 3A for the last eight years, and told her "next year you'll have 3B and it'll be a tonic all round". Well she broke down and burst into tears, said she wouldn't take them and threatened to leave. And after one term with 3B, she did leave.'

These efforts were apt to be defeated. In three of the ten schools the Heads did nothing to disturb a settled order of 'A' and 'C' teachers, except when posts fell vacant. In the other seven, they shuffled whom they could, and occasionally fought a pitched battle with an established 'A' stream teacher. Mr. Davies remembered how he'd managed to move his deputy head from 4A to 4B:

'I told him, I'm having no arguments or discussion; tomorrow you take 4B. I was most upset about the trouble it caused, but I put Miss Bell in charge of 4A, and she worked like a Trojan—got marvellous results. No new methods, just sheer hard work and no favourites. She went round that class rapping their knuckles with a ruler, and do you know she was just as likely to hit the brightest boy in the class as to hit the dullest. The children wor-shipped her. Her discipline was perfect. She took that class for 12 years until she died last winter.'

It was frequently like this. In every change around, strong teachers re-established themselves in the crucial position—especially 4A, the class which contained tomorrow's elite: and which, for the teacher, usually led to a Headship.

'It's only human. We can't help feeling that if the children from our class go to grammar school, it's kudos for us—they're our *property.*'

The Headteachers fought their sporadic battles against the 'streaming' of teachers—but they lost. The disposition of graded

posts and the siting of some 'C' streams in inferior accommodation, suggested that they accepted the hopelessness of seeking for much talent in 'B' or 'C' children.[1]

Pressure from parents

No parents from these schools were interviewed. Only two
of the schools had a parent-teacher organization, though all the
others held Open Days or parents' evenings. Three Heads had
closed down a parent-teacher association. All said that it was
dominated by 'A' stream parents whom they saw anyway. One
Head closed his down because 'it was no more than a whist
drive club'. Two (in middle class suburbs) acted because they
resented parents commenting on the internal running of the
school, and because of pressure from prominent parents to get
their children in the 'A' class. Mr. Gregory claimed that when
he took over his school, the previous Head had utterly collapsed
against this force and 'there were 60 children in the top 'A'
stream!'

All the Heads reported that 'A' stream parents strongly
favoured streaming, that 'B' or 'C' parents accepted it or
'didn't care'. The hardest problems for a Headteacher came in
schools with a substantial middle-class intake, where a number
of articulate parents found their child in the 'B' stream. Schools
like this—with up to 50 per cent. of the pupils going to grammar school—did score a number of places with 'B' children.
All could illustrate at length the movement of middle-class
parents into their 'zone'.

'The house agent often tells me that parents come to him asking
for houses within the "zone", so that their children come here.'

'When they arrive in the town, they come and ask if I've room.

---

[1] *Transferring streams*: Of course there was always the chance of transferring a child from one stream to another. All Heads stressed this flexibility, but a check of the previous year's records showed that the average
rate of transfer moved from 8 per cent. in the first year to 2 per cent. in
the last year. Transfer was difficult, firstly because 'I don't like demotions,
only promotions—I push them up when I can, but I don't like putting one
down in their place.' Secondly, because it was common experience that the
top 'B' children were difficult to absorb into an 'A' stream. They couldn't
always readjust to the change of pace and emphasis, sometimes struggled
unhappily at the bottom of the new class and had to be returned to the
lower stream. It was all very similar to Honey Bell.

That's it—and if they have any trouble, they bring out the Education Act and this Authority always backs down. If they couldn't get in here, they'd send them off to private school.'

Though the law gives parents certain rights of choice, a determined authority—either in a spirit of social fairness or of bureaucratic rigidity—can permanently obstruct them. But usually the problem is avoided by expanding school accommodation in response not only to population shifts, but also to this other line of pressure. A *modus vivendi* is reached so that the number of frustrated middle class parents is very much reduced. This is helped even more because the oldest primary schools were built for working class populations in the nineteenth century. When new schools have to be built, it is often to meet the needs of middle class suburbs which had, until recently, depended on private education.

These ten schools gave Honey Bell a small context. All shared that school's beliefs in 'kinds' of children; none had its magnificent modern buldings, or the *panache* with which it carried off the venture. Certainly the 'C' children at Honey Bell were fortunate in not being 'C' children at one or two of the other schools. And Mr. Rivers' 'B' children were being given something much more valuable, with their animal farm, than the 'B' children under one Headship here, where their distinct privilege and training was to wash up the teachers' dinner plates, whilst 'A' children acted as supervising prefects and 'C' children 'couldn't be trusted' with any jobs.

At Honey Bell each child *was* trusted and valued. They were never treated as less than human beings, but they were treated as 'kinds' of human beings, and the quantity and nature of excellence that the school nurtured was pre-determined by its technique of streaming and the dense mass of custom, values and endorsements behind it.

Ten unstreamed schools

But what other ways exist in England of organizing the education of young children? The majority of primary schools that can stream, do stream—and a personal impression based on visits to smaller schools suggests that most of these also 'stream' in the sense that 'bright' groups are picked out at 6 or 7 and offered a separate education from the body of children.

But 27 of the schools sampled in chapter two were un-streamed, and twelve of these were visited. From 10 it was possible to gather reasonable data for they had been unstreamed, on average, for six years; the remaining two had only just un-streamed. These 10 schools were all in areas in which some form of comprehensive education was available to some children. They faced '11 plus', but the pressures from this were markedly reduced.

Four of the ten schools were on totally working-class housing estates built in recent years. Here there was hardly any impact on the school from parents, and the Head was undisputed Lord and Master. Five other schools were new, and had never been streamed. Here again the Head had been remarkably free from pressures whilst he was establishing this new form of organization. The tenth school was in the Leicestershire experimental area.

Apart from the slackening of external academic and social pressures, the unstreamed schools differed from the ten streamed ones in being much more overcrowded. They had an average of 39 pupils per class compared to 35 pupils in the streamed schools. The unstreamed schools were also less successful in the previous year's eleven plus—though they were above the average of their area.

TABLE 34

PERCENTAGE OF CHILDREN GOING ON TO GRAMMAR SCHOOL

	10 *Streamed Schools*	10 *Unstreamed Schools*
Average percentage of children at grammar school in these areas	23%	21%
Percentage of children at the schools who went on to grammar school in the previous year	37%	23%
Highest percentage recorded at any one school	50%	29%
Lowest percentage recorded at any one school	18%	7%

These 11 plus scores may or may not reflect differences in academic standards, they certainly do reflect variations in provision from area to area. Often they mirror differences in the social background of the two types of schools.

Some of the Heads were quick to point out that their achievement must be considered against the local background. One school in Lancashire was on a vast new housing estate. On the fringes of this totally working class estate were five huge factories. It was believed that no child had gone to University from this district since the estates were built in 1946.[1]

In Yorkshire, one Headmaster pointed out that of the 128 pupils who stayed to lunch at his school, 32 had it free of charge. 'And the Probation Officer was in here yesterday to say that if the Ackroyd kids wanted to know where their father was, tell them he's gone cabbage-picking in Lincolnshire. In fact he's in jail again. He's usually home three months of the year—just gets out long enough to put his wife in the family way and then he's back in again. Last year, I can tell you, we had seven fathers in jail at the same time.' This was the school in which 7 per cent. of the pupils were successful in 11 plus.

Inside the schools

Two of the Heads prevented us from seeing their schools in action. The other eight were open and friendly, and quite experienced in dealing with possibly hostile visitors:

'Because this school is unstreamed, some parents get it into their head that this is a do-as-you-like school. I had one mother in last November who was worried because she thought this was a do-as-you-like place, and she wanted her boy to pass his 11 plus, be given some hard discipline and not allowed to do as he liked. So I took her to the glass courtyard in the middle of the school and said: "Look, we can see 300 children from here. They're all working, aren't they? All busy, orderly, learning. Nobody's doing--as-they-like. I don't seem to hear the sound of breaking glass

---

[1] In *The Home and The School*, Douglas, J. W. B. arrays some impressive statistical evidence on this question, and concludes that 'children at schools with a good academic record get more grammar school places than their test scores at eleven years would seem to entitle them, whereas those at schools with a poor record get 37 per cent. fewer. These figures in each instance make allowances for the social selection of the pupils and the difference in the local availability of grammar school places.'

and screaming teachers." But it had absolutely no effect on her. She felt the school was somehow *wrong.'*

This school, like most of the others, was certainly different. Children's work was plentifully displayed in all the unstreamed classrooms, whereas in the streamed schools the 'A' classes had lots to show, but all except one of the 'C' classes had very little. Art was not only more plentiful but more imaginative in the unstreamed schools, and there was no way of telling whether the makers of some of the most attractive models—a huge, grotesque dwarf with the shoulders slightly wrong, a purple and silver pottery owl squatting on a scarlet rock—would have been 'A', 'B' or 'C' children elsewhere.

The effects of unstreaming by itself were difficult to access, since in most schools it had not happened 'by itself'. It went with a different approach to learning, to discipline, to what gifts should be valued. Most unstreamed schools gave much prominence to art, and some of them to music and drama too. The teachers concentrated less on bookwork, less on an education which was only intellectual. Their teaching was aimed not only at the intellect, but at the senses and the emotions. It was both imaginative and practical. Mr. Capey was teaching his class the geography of rivers. He had taken them down to a nearby stream and standing them on the bank had asked them *why* there was a stream in that place and in no other. Back in the classroom he pursued his lesson by having children pour water through plant pots, some containing sand, others containing garden soil and others packed with clay. The children were measuring the time it took the water to seep through, and writing it up in their notebooks. On the blackboard were key words that weaker children might want to use, yet not know how to spell. The quality of the children's work varied considerably, but they were co-operating and not competing with each other. A wide spread of skills was being used—practical, analytic, illustrative, literary—and the children had different levels of talent at each. It was more like a well-organized workshop, than a desk-centred classroom.

At most of the streamed schools the desks faced the teacher in equal ranks. Occasionally the children sat in them according to rank order in their regular tests. But the unstreamed schools usually had desks in small informal groups, so that children faced other children. The dominating teacher was no longer the classroom's focus.

The unstreamed schools certainly had problems of backwardness to face. The most successful schools were those which concentrated heavily on teaching children to read at the age of seven, and followed this up by withdrawing single children or small groups from the class for special coaching. The assumption that all the children probably *could* read, put into practice by an initial blitz on reading followed by small group sessions, underpinned much of the later success of the unstreamed school. The difference with most streamed schools here, lay not so much in reading technique but in the basic belief that the children could be taught, and that there was no need to tolerate this part of the 'C' stream problem.

Other parts of the 'C' stream problem—indiscipline, hostility to work, and so on—had disappeared because such children were not brought together as a class, where attitudes grew more stubborn or intense. Split up among other boys and girls—stable, excited, co-operative—they received a quite different social education.

'For some of these children this was the first time they'd been really stimulated. They overwhelmed, flooded the teacher with work done. Then it became too much to cope with and the teachers had to have the children marking a lot of their own work—that set some of my old-style teachers worrying. They wouldn't believe—until they had to try it—that children *could* mark so much of their own work.'

Why had the schools been unstreamed?

Most of the Heads gave primarily social reasons for unstreaming their schools—matters of tone, spirit and atmosphere.

'At the last school of which I was Head, the "A" classes were all right—bright and alert, up to the mark, interested and keen. But "B" and "C" classes were dull and lethargic. You see, the "A" children were the tops at everything—prizes, prefects, sport. It was as if the "B" and "C" classes had nothing to try for: even in School Prayers they wouldn't really join in. You couldn't properly get them even to sing.'

Two of the Heads saw unstreaming as being part of a more individual approach to teaching:

'At other schools where I was it was almost a disgrace to take a "C" class and an honour to take an "A" class. I saw my Heads put beginners in "C" classes and experienced men in "A" classes: and "C"-mindedness in a child or teacher is a disastrous thing. People talk about streaming or unstreaming as if it's in a vacuum, but it's not. Unstreaming this school was a way of getting away from class teaching, class-mindedness, of any sort, a way of making my teachers accept children as individuals moving at different rates.'

One Head had never thought about unstreaming until he attended a Ministry of Education course and talked these matters over with Inspectors and other Heads. No doubt some of the streamed school Heads quoted in chapter 3 would be suspicious of this as catching on to a fashion or carving a future career in the Inspectorate. Finally, one Head claimed that his decision to unstream had been clinched by a passing conversation with a neighbour's child.

'I'm glad you got through 11 plus, Raymond. How did your friend get on?'
'Oh him! *He* didn't get through. He's in with the yobs.'

Except in this kind of way, none of the Heads gave academic reasons for the change, and none claimed it would increase the attainment of the 'A' stream child. What they did feel was that it would improve self-respect, increase co-operation and kindliness, create an atmosphere in which all children could work happily, and compel the teacher to recognize the diversity of children's gifts.

The Heads who were given the job of starting a new school in new buildings had little difficulty in creating an unstreamed school. They were starting something, not overturning something. But the Heads who wanted to unstream a school which was already streamed had a very difficult task. Mr. Carpenter in the Midlands began by unstreaming his third year as an experiment, partly because the third year teachers were mildly co-operative whereas the rest of his staff was unconvinced or hostile. The experiment was a disaster. The children came from streamed classes and would return to streamed classes. Most of the staff were not in favour of the one year experiment. Neither teachers, nor parents, nor children liked it, and the consequence was twelve months' unhappiness and confusion. Mr. Carpenter had to abandon his scheme for several years, and then try again. This time he began at the bottom and unstreamed his 7 year-olds. He worked hard at the problem of teaching them all to read and the following year when they moved up, he built on his success and still didn't stream them. In this way the school was gradually unstreamed by a four-year process. His teachers gathered confidence or moved to other schools, and he didn't have to deal with his most formidable opponents—the teachers of the 11 year-olds—until three-quarters of the school was unstreamed, and three-quarters of his staff behind it. It was exactly this method that was followed with success by all the other unstreamed Heads. Yet even so, unstreaming a school could often mean difficult—even ugly—scenes.

'When I went into her classroom, she totally ignored me. It was a *disgrace* that she, an "A" teacher, should take that class.'

The teachers who remained all reported that unstreamed teaching was harder than streamed work: lessons had to be organized with more care, especially the details of individual and small group work. In return they found teaching more interesting, and often exciting. Work was varied, old routines could no longer be followed, and the children were more co-operative. New teachers coming to such a school, straight from training college, spoke of them as a stiff but pleasurable challenge, and seemed to accept the unstreamed situation without too much difficulty.

Heads who unstreamed faced difficulties from parents. This was especially so in *mixed* social areas where streaming had previously separated most working class from most middle-class children. Several Heads spoke of annoyed parents coming to the school to protest. At one, middle class parents had approached their M.P. and persuaded him to tackle the Minister of Education. At another they had lobbied their Education Officer; and here and there an occasional child had been withdrawn and sent to a private school.

In one-class districts, and with new schools, there was far less trouble. Parents either accepted unstreaming or were indifferent to it. Or even misunderstood it. A Yorkshire Headmaster said that even though his school had been unstreamed for six years, parents did not accept that there was no such grading—and it was popularly believed in the district that children taught on the second floor of the school were distinctly brighter than children whose classrooms were on the ground floor. In a school in Essex, a Head had a similar story of how parents remembered exactly which classroom had contained the 11 plus scholarship children for 20 years, and politely disbelieved him when he said that boys and girls in that room were now no more able than the rest. Heads could unstream schools, but not local society.

Are unstreamed schools academically worse?

Almost all the teachers in streamed schools had insisted that the academic standards of able children dropped in an unstreamed class. Most of them thought—both in the sample discussed in Chapter 3, and in the ten streamed schools described earlier in this Chapter—that the academic standards of all children would decline.

This conflicts with the small amount of evidence we have on this subject in Britain. Much of this is highly indecisive, but a suggestive piece of research is reported by Dr. J. C. Daniels[1] in which he compares in some detail, academic progress in two streamed and two unstreamed schools. He reports that progress in reading, English and arithmetic was more rapid for *all* children in the unstreamed school, but particularly for the weakest children.

I did not myself have the resources to undertake a full enquiry into the academic stature of unstreamed schools, and for this we will have to wait for the results of the major enquiry now being undertaken by the National Foundation for Educational Research. But as a small pointer I tried collecting and

---

[1] Daniels, J. C. 'The Effects of Streaming in Primary School', *Brit. Journal Educ. Psychol.* February, 1961 and June, 1962. Previous research into this subject is very usefully summarised by Yates, A., and Pidgeon, D. A. 'The Effects of Streaming' *Education Research,* November 1959, and Rudd, W. . A., 'The Effects of Streaming: A Further Contribution' in *Education Research,* June, 1960.

comparing the results of tests in reading. This approach had many weaknesses. First of all, the unstreamed schools did not have many such records. Secondly, I did not know how well tests had been administered, scored or recorded. Thirdly, it was extremely hard to match groups of children. I finally decided to make a small attempt at academic comparison and to follow as closely as I could the matching method used by Dr. Daniels in his research. This can be illustrated by the first comparison I was able to make.

A recently unstreamed school in Hertfordshire had reading records of 8 and 9 year old children, who had been taught in the streamed classes at the school, and these could be contrasted with the records of similar children's progress now the school was unstreamed. Both groups of children had taken the same test (Schonell 'B' Sentence Reading Test) at the end of their first year in the school, and also at the end of their second year. There were 88 children in the streamed year and 101 in the unstreamed year, and at about the age of 8 their progress was as follows:

TABLE 35

READING ATTAINMENT AT THE END OF THE
FIRST JUNIOR SCHOOL YEAR

Reading Quotient	*Children in Streamed Classes*	*Children in Unstreamed Classes*
130+	18	19
120+	11	11
110+	14	13
100+	19	19
90+	13	25
80+	7	14
70+	0	0
70−	7	0
Total	88	101
Mean	109.1	108.9
Standard Deviation	20.3	17.7

After one year in the streamed classes, 7 children were very backward (reading quotients of less than 70), whereas there were no such children left after one year in the unstreamed classes. I could not tell whether this was due to the teaching, the streaming, the class size, or the background and ability of the children who had come in those particular years.

Following Dr. Daniels I now gave a number to each child. I then took a list of random numbers, and using that, struck out one 'unstreamed' child with a reading quotient of more than 130. This left me with two matched groups of 18 children each who were above the highest attainment level. I did nothing about the groups of children with quotients of more than 120 since there were already 11 in each group. But I removed one 'streamed' child from the next group down by this method and so on until I had the following sample.

TABLE 36

SAMPLE OF 162 CHILDREN AT THE END OF THEIR
FIRST JUNIOR SCHOOL YEAR

Reading Quotient	Children in Streamed Classes	Children in Unstreamed Classes
130+	18	18
120+	11	11
110+	13	13
100+	19	19
90+	13	13
80+	7	7
70+	0	0
70−	0	0
Total	81	81

This procedure gave a sample matched for attainment, though I knew nothing else of the children.

I followed the progress of this sample until the end of their second junior school year when they were about 9 years old. Again they had taken the identical reading test. These were the results:

113

TABLE 37

SAMPLE OF 162 CHILDREN AT THE END OF THEIR
SECOND JUNIOR SCHOOL YEAR

Reading Quotient	Children in Streamed Classes	Children in Unstreamed Classes
130+	18	26
120+	14	16
110+	13	14
100+	8	13
90+	16	7
80+	10	4
70+	2	1
70−	0	0
Total	81	81

In the unstreamed class the obviously able children had done rather better; the weakest children had improved remarkably and the average attainment of the whole class had been lifted. This was in line with the results reported by Daniels, and it may be that, contrary to the views of most teachers, unstreaming produces academically superior results—even with the child who would otherwise attend an 'A' class. Of course it would be rash to come to any such conclusions on this evidence: the weaknesses of the method are plain, and the numbers involved are tiny. But the suggestion is interesting.

I was twice again able to compare reading progress in a school when it was streamed and then when it was unstreamed. Both gave similar results—the near disappearance of the 'C' child so far as reading was concerned, and a small improvement in the average and top scores. It is not surprising that *any* change of system creates new standards in a school, especially since it may be involved with a change of Head and other staff. A fairer comment on unstreaming would be a comparison of quite different streamed and unstreamed schools. I attempted this, but there were only sufficient records in reading for me to be able to make six comparisons. There were never adequate records to make comparisons in any other subject.

Four of these six comparisons followed the previous pattern —unstreamed classes helping all children improve their attainment, but specially helping the children on the bottom rungs. The remaining two comparisons showed ņo real difference between either system. It must be remembered that I was comparing such unstreamed schools as I could find with a sample of streamed schools chosen for me by the local authorities—and clearly the streamed schools were chosen precisely because of their high attainments in these matters.

Criticisms of unstreamed schools

Though many of the unstreamed schools were exciting places to visit, certain criticisms were plain. First of all, two of the Heads politely prevented anyone looking round the classrooms and talking to teachers and children. My feeling here was that both Heads had made an organizational change—streaming to unstreaming—but little more. I suspect there had been no change of values or teaching technique in these schools, and the attempt to teach and think in the old way, but with unstreamed classes was causing considerable confusion. The merely administrative change had not been anything like enough to solve the problems of how to teach the children as individuals.

Secondly, this conflict between two approaches to teaching was still causing difficulty in some of the other unstreamed schools visited. For example, one near Liverpool still maintained some of the old rituals. When the Head or a visitor entered a class, the children rose, stood at attention and raising their hands to their heads, as though taking caps off, chanted lethargically 'Good morning, Mrs. Curtis Brown' or whatever the name was. At Honey Bell such ceremonies were carried off with vigour; here they were flat and bewildering. On the academic side, there were sometimes similar confusions. Two of the unstreamed Heads were distinctly pre-selecting grammar school candidates six months before the examination and giving them very special teaching in speed work and 11 plus tests. This was never publicly mentioned. Again it was hopelessly furtive and half-hearted compared to Honey Bell.

Thirdly, many of the schools in abandoning streaming had abandoned other things that could have been of value to them.

The clearest example were tests of any kind. These were taboo in some schools, presumably because they were so associated with early streaming. It may have been a good thing that the children were not now so constantly graded, but it did mean that Heads often had little precise idea of their pupils' attainment or local weaknesses. There was a strong case for using reputable attainment and diagnostic tests, even in an unstreamed school, to spot and chart individual successes and difficulties. There is a world of difference between knowing about children's strengths and weaknesses early, and putting them into separate classes based on those variations.

Fourthly, I came across kinds of 'unstreaming' which had some of the unhappier characteristics of streaming. A rare example was a school which divided its children up on entry according to friendship patterns. In this sense children who had all grown up together in the same working class street were 'friends' and went into one class; other children arriving at the same school from a group of prosperous bungalows were also 'friends' and entered the other class. This too-crude use of the 'friendship' method produced a mild form of 'A' and 'B' streaming. But more common was the system where the Head had decided to put all the children born in the first third of the year into one class, regardless of ability. He then put the children born in the next third of the year into a second class and so on. This kind of division is something that underpins normal streaming as the survey in Chapter 2 illustrated. Such a school, singing hymns in morning assembly, looked oddly like a streamed school, for when a streamed school assembled it was sometimes possible to see the difference in average height between an 'A' class and a 'C' class: slightly older, better-fed 'A' children were that bit taller. Unstreamed schools using age as their divider presented the same spectacle—not only was there a regular drop in height between different years, but also between classes in a year, like a run of long shallow steps. The same shallow, but clear differences showed up in the children's work, too. This kind of 'unstreaming' usually began, I think, in genuine error: Heads did not foresee the importance of small age differences institutionalized in class form. It may have continued because it was a mild form of insurance against low scores in 11 plus: the eldest class kept the annual pass percentage high. One Head said quite openly:

'Education in our country is a rat race, and naturally you want to win as many places at grammar school as you can. I don't accept the rat race conception of education, that's why I've unstreamed. But I can't get over the fact that 11 plus is there and it's important. So non-streaming's bound to be thwarted like this, until society abolishes selection.'

This half-way method was always described as 'unstreaming', and usually went along with the change in teaching techniques that I came to expect in other non-streamed schools.

The criticisms I list above are not surprising. One would expect a gradation between streamed and unstreamed schools rather than a sudden cleavage. And inevitably there would be hard problems of how many of the old ceremonies and expectations should be abandoned. Yet it was a little disheartening to meet Heads who felt that the merely organizational switch to unstreaming was the end of the matter. It was also disheartening for Heads to realise that their unstreamed school was hemmed in by a streamed society.

Two preliminary points emerged from these sometimes uncertain, pathfinder attempts to build a different kind of school. The first is immediate and practical: each of these Heads was working largely by himself, he was often repeating errors made by other non-streaming Heads, falling into mistakes and tangles that could have been avoided had practical advice or demonstration been available. If we accept that Heads have a right to unstream their schools, then there is a case for giving them instruction on how best to do this, how to deal with staff problems, and how to help teachers change their techniques. It would not be hard for the Ministry or Local Authorities to set up practical and thorough courses for this purpose; courses that must, above all, take the Heads into other schools. The utter isolation of Headteachers is saddening, and extraordinarily inefficient.

The second point that emerged turned on the old question of: must we first change schools before we can change society, or must we change society before we can change schools? This formulation was put to me in school after school, and phrased

117

J

like that it can paralyse action, or sanction inaction by its seeming hopelessness. But these are not alternatives, and in a small way the unstreamed schools were showing that if 'change' is your desire, you can take small steps along both roads.

Summary

In this chapter ten streamed schools, chosen by their education authority, were compared to ten unstreamed schools drawn from the sample in chapter two. The streamed schools shared the basic values and system of Honey Bell. Some of the 'A' classes seemed particularly excellent in almost every respect, but few of them were as successful with their 'B' or 'C' classes as Mr. Rivers had been. Often the 'C' class was low in attainment, and markedly demoralised: possibly its very classroom was separated from the school proper. 'A' classes were in the charge of older, more experienced teachers. Nine out of the ten deputy heads taught 'A' streams. Heads were often uneasy about this and in favour of a transfer of teachers and pupils from class to class, but such transfer was never great because of the gap that opened up between 'A', 'B', or 'C' pupils, and because strong teachers established in key 'A' stream posts were hard to budge. These ten schools, like Honey Bell, selected gifted children early and divided their pupils up into three broad kinds of ability. Honey Bell was more vigorous in this policy than other streamed schools, and though it enclosed each stream in a similar net of expectations, it carried this off with more *panache*. The future academics, craftsmen, and labourers whom it produced kept their own 'stream', but within that developed their approved talents more thoroughly.

Compared to the ten streamed schools, the unstreamed sample were mostly new schools or schools in working class areas. In order to flourish, 11 plus selection had to slacken or disappear, and pressure from parents to be minimal. On the whole they sent a smaller percentage of children to grammar school, but were sited in areas which had a smaller percentage of grammar schools anyway. Two of the Heads did not allow a full survey of their school. The remaining eight schools were, as a group, more crowded yet more relaxed in atmosphere than the streamed schools. There was not the drive, competition or tension common in the streamed schools; more time was devoted to music, art and drama, and rather less to the desk-work of arithmetic and English exercises. It was hard to compare the two groups of schools, since so much more than unstreaming distinguished them. The teaching techniques were usually different—with less class work, and much more small group and individual work. They were schools in which children frequently *surprised* their teachers by some new interest or success. Because there was a difference of values, techniques, expectation and organization between the two types of school, academic comparisons are difficult to judge. Furthermore, the school records were sometimes of doubtful value. Allowing this, there were eight cases where the reading progress of a year group of streamed children could be compared with a year group of unstreamed children. Two of these comparisons showed little difference between either method. The other six follow the pattern reported by Dr. Daniels: all children improved somewhat in the unstreamed schools, but the weakest children gained most. Besides creating higher academic standards, unstreamed schools had a narrower spread of attainment. The long 'C' stream tail had disappeared.

Before making these comparisons I was already doubtful of the value of streaming, though impressed by the vigour which sometimes went into a classic streamed school such as Honey Bell. I had little experience of large, unstreamed schools, though I liked the free and friendly atmosphere I had known in schools too small to consider streaming. By the end of this survey several personal impressions had clarified. First, though an academic comparison between the two systems now seems to me to be extremely subtle and full of pitfalls, I think there are reasonable pointers suggesting that unstreaming can abolish the 'C' stream tail. It may be that otherwise there is academically little difference between the two methods.

But there certainly were considerable *social* difference between them. I did not know how to measure atmosphere or mood but I record as an impression that unstreamed schools replaced competition by helpfulness, and had re-created in large schools the friendly atmosphere I noted in small ones. For example, in most of the streamed schools it was an offence for one child to turn to another for aid with an arithmetical problem.

This was 'copying' and to be punished. Yet in most of the unstreamed schools this turning of one child to another was constantly encouraged by the teachers, and rewarded with small words of praise. I never spoke to a child who had moved from a streamed to an unstreamed school but I imagine it could be an astonishing experience. Not only the system changes, but the importance of certain lessons, the very position where the teacher stands in class, the relationship of child to child, the whole ethic of the room.

This was the social difference as the child met it. But to the adult observer the main distinction lay in the development of children's gifts. Streamed schools produced a predetermined number of gifted children: the kind of giftedness they encouraged was also predetermined. But the unstreamed schools were less predictable, more varied. They were schools in which children surprised teachers. This summary is perhaps too generous to their many small faults; but at their best moments unstreamed schools drew *more* of the child into classroom activity and helped bring into life the multiplicity, the often odd mixtures of abilities that boys and girls had in them.

I was impressed by many of the achievements of streamed schools that I saw, and did not feel that the comparisons made here were between ten *bad* schools and ten *good* ones. But I was more impressed by the *potentiality* of the unstreamed schools. There were schools in which, at their finest, there were few bars to the amount or kind of excellence that they nurtured. The streamed schools were like magnificent machines able to refine precisely limited amounts of gold, silver and baser metals. But the unstreamed schools had the potentialities of yeast which, under good conditions, reduplicates.

7

PROPOSALS

THIS book began with a personal story. As a primary school teacher I had the normal run of failure and success teaching boys and girls in 'A', 'B' and 'C' classes. I was myself a kind of 'A' child, grown up—for the 'B' and 'C' children do not become teachers. So I suppose that in ways I did not question I was more attuned to the 'A' classes and they to me than either realised. Yet teaching streamed children was a puzzling experience, if only because the roots of their problems lay far outside the classroom. It was perplexing to encounter creative children in 'C' classes and tidyminded but less enterprising children in 'A' classes. Especially so when you knew that selection was open and fair, and that by no conceivable method could Martin who, at moments, painted and wrote with such clarity ('The sky was thrush egg blue with a few mistletoe white clouds scudding across the burning sun') be set on the road to grammar school and university within the system as it stands. For along with the bursts of creative energy went wretched arithmetic, absences from school, indifference to grammar school ambitions. And so many of the other children, if you knew them well, were at once individuals, unique fusions of qualities, and at the same time, types—'A's or 'C's pliant to the pressure of parents and teachers. Possibly I might have learned more of society's creation of the 'types' it desired if I had set about an enquiry into 'intelligence'; or if I had probed more deeply and narrowly into parents' desires or teachers' values. But as it was, streaming looked like the clue to thread the maze.

It did not do that. It led over ground that was new to me and uncovered some puzzles along the way. But there the thread ran out, leaving me nearer the heart of the maze, with some sense of which avenues were still open and which were end-stopped. But both the evidence I have and the argument I draw from it must admit very large gaps and passages of ambiguous interpretation. The chapter that follows begins by recording what has emerged about streaming, and offers some practical conclusions.

Does streaming aid learning?

The 655 teachers, questioned in Chapter two generally believed that streaming was essential if academic standards were to be preserved. Most expected a sudden and serious decline in the

TABLE 38

Average Standard Deviation

STANDARD DEVIATION ON FIVE TESTS TAKEN BY
13 YEAR OLDS IN TWELVE COUNTRIES

quality of work at unstreamed schools. Yet this had not happened, and apart from general impressions it was possible to make eight small comparisons. These had their weaknesses, but two showed no differences, and on six, unstreamed children scored more highly. This was similar to Dr. J. C. Daniels' findings. Before Daniels, research into the subject had been highly indecisive; so much so that a summary[1] of it by Yates and Pidgeon of the National Foundation for Educational Research in 1959 concluded. 'It is clear from this review of the sparse research that has been devoted to the problem of streaming that it is possible neither to justify the criticisms that have been levelled against it, nor to prove that streaming is a desirable and effective form of organisation.' But in 1962, a year after Daniels' results were published, D. A. Pidgeon had the opportunity to co-operate in an international enquiry into the educational achievements of thirteen year old children in twelve different countries.[2] These children were tested in 5 different subjects; and the *spread* of scores by the English pupils was by far the largest. Scotland came next.

No country outside the United Kingdom 'streamed' children, and Pidgeon felt that this large spread of scores in the English sample reflected our system of streamed classes within a streamed system. This adds a little to the evidence suggesting that streaming in itself, and the beliefs that lie behind it, may be partly responsible for our long 'C' stream tail.[3]

My own feeling is that we still know very little about the academic effects of streaming: the evidence we have is vulnerable in many ways. Further, no one has shown that it is even *possible* to make the strictest kind of comparison, when so much else, from teachers' techniques to parents' attitudes is involved. But we do know that unstreamed schools are *no worse* academically than their predecessors. And we have pretty reasonable pointers that they can be better for all children, and certainly so for the less able or less fortunate.

Professor Vernon has calculated that if normal shifts in measured intelligence were allowed for, 40 per cent. of primary

[1] Yates, A. and Pidgeon, D. A., 'The Effects of Streaming' in *Educational Research,* November, 1959. See also Rudd, W. G. A. 'The Effects of Streaming: A Further Contribution' in *Educational Research,* June, 1960.

[2] *Educational Achievements of Thirteen-Year-Olds in Twelve Countries* (UNESCO Institute of Education, Hamburg). There are weaknesses in the samples drawn by some countries which may affect these results.

[3] After this was written some very important research on streaming was published by J. W. B. Douglas in *The Home and The School* (1964). This is discussed in Appendix 2.

schools *ought* to transfer streams. No teachers imagine that this happens, or would happen, except in the most extraordinary situation: the research quoted earlier suggests that a transfer of five or six per cent. a year may be normal. And after 11, if it becomes a matter of transferring from one school to another, the chances shrink further. Here Vernon estimates that 'even with the use of the most adequate selective instruments it remains true that in some areas up to forty-five per cent. of the children in the eleven plus age group may be classified as borderline'. So far as can be seen, the national transfer rate between grammar school and others is about one per cent.[1]

All these calculations are of course within the terms of the system as it stands, and make assumptions about ambition and the nature of intelligence that can be challenged. But they are enough to illustrate the rigor mortis that easily besets a streamed system: the inbuilt finality of judgment, so hard to overmaster. Given the society and teachers we have, a technique like streaming will always rigidify.

Does streaming help children socially?

The academic grading is also a social ABC. Here we are near the boundaries of the measurable, and evidence is more double-edged, vulnerable to the tug and flow of our personal experience. A few things are beyond question: streaming reflects social background, privilege, accident and handicap. Middle class children move into 'A' streams, working class children into 'B' and 'C's. The homes where the parents are separated, or where one is dead, or unemployed, or crippled, usually belong to 'B' and 'C' children. And along with this division by background or fortune, comes the division into separate spheres of expectation. This may arise from the school, as at Honey Bell, where the 'A's were taught on the assumption of academic skills, the 'C's on the assumption of manual skills.[2] Or it may

---

[1] In the two cities where I was able to do a spot check it was less than one eighth of one per cent. Both places divided their children entirely into grammar school and secondary modern pupils.

[2] Research suggests that children do *not* divide into those with practised skills and those with theoretical ones. See Elmgren, J. *School and Psychology* and Husen, T. 'Educational Structure and the Development of Ability', in Halsey, A. H. *Ability and Educational Opportunity*, O.E.E.D., 1961.

stem from the neighbourhood where the parents of the children in all streams accept that there are perceptible kinds of children. ('It's in us British'). Or it may come from children themselves, adjusting their personalities and goals to the 'A', 'B' or 'C' expectation. The 'C' child is soon unconcerned with grammar school ambitions and the life and values he vaguely associates with it: many of his idols—pop singer or star footballer—found room at the top without leaping hurdles of 11 plus and beyond. And he is not always looking for room at the top anyway.

Children know something of this. At Honey Bell, 'beauty' was streamed and the group of older Yorkshire children quoted in Chapter 4 had strong views on their status prospects ('Practically everybody treats you like a scruff.'). They accept their lot, and at eleven plus have a sober idea of their chances in life. For example, Dr. Hilde Himmelweit once reported a study[2] in which 63 per cent. of working class boys selected from grammar school expected to rise socially quite a way beyond their fathers; but only 12 per cent. of the boys in secondary modern schools felt this. This knowledge of the social consequences of streaming and eleven plus can be compared with the selfknowledge of American children. In their more flexible system, research consistently shows children aspiring to positions, many of which will be beyond their reach.[3] This can be interpreted as American 'phantasy' as against British 'realism'. It can also be seen as American opportunity as against British restriction. Either way it suggests that children *know* the social as well as academic nature of streaming, and that teachers who

---

[1] A small piece of confirmatory record is reported by C. J. Willig who on a sample of 200 children aged nine to ten, reports that 'there was virtually no social interaction between 'A' and 'B' classes'. When the children were offered a choice, almost all 'A' children wanted to remain in an 'A' class if transferred to another school, 94 per cent. of the 'B' children from middle class areas wanted an 'A' position and 54 per cent. of the 'B' children from working class districts wanted it. Willig, C. J. 'Social Implications of Streaming in the Junior School' in *Educational Research*, February, 1962.

[2] Himmelweit, H. T., et al., 'Views of Adolescents on some Aspects of Social Class Structure,' *British Journal of Sociology*, June, 1952.

[3] See Turner, R. H., 'Modes of Social Ascent through Education: Sponsored and Contest Mobility' reprinted in Halsey, A. H., Floud, J., and Anderson, C. A. (eds), *Education, Economy and Society*.

feel children are quite unconscious of it ('Lot of bunkum talked by long-haired intellectuals in this field') are mistaken.

There is one curious point about the social effects of streaming. 'A' classes, segregated and streamlined, were an elite in training. But 'C' classes, separate and inward-turning, were almost a text-book illustration of how to create the culture of the gang. None of these 'C' classes were filled with hooligans; yet all the necessary conditions for the embryo gang were provided by the school. The 'C' children of Honey Bell had decided at eleven that they preferred 'C' stream to 'A' stream beauty; already they had their own distinctive 'pop' idols. In a few years their own hair styles and clothes would have the bonding effect of a uniform. There is nothing to be troubled by here, unless there is also the bonding effect of despair, failure, and sterile hooliganism. Secondary school sometimes brings that. This would be a vast and complex connection to illustrate or prove; certainly beyond the range of any evidence I can muster. But I understand that the most delinquent group in recent years were those children whose 5th to 7th birthdays fell during war years: clearly crucial years for social behaviour.[1] It is possible that being 'C' streamed at 7 could have a lasting effect on some children analagous to the disturbances of war-time life. Especially with tight groups who are separated from the social patterns and even the language of values transmitted by groups of untroubled children chosen for 'A' streams.[2] This is speculation, but I think there are enough patches of evidence to suggest that streaming may have some small connection with fostering future delinquency.

Streaming and the Teacher

Streaming has a distinct social effect. But it *is* itself a social effect: and one difficulty throughout this string of enquiries has been the intangible importance of teachers' values and parents' values. These are harder to document than organizational

---

[1] Wilkins, L. T., *Delinquent Generations*. Also Cohen, A. K., *Culture of the Gang* and Sutherland, E. H., *Principles of Criminology*.

[2] In the unstreamed situation groupings are very much looser and children, who would otherwise be separated, mix together. See Miller, T. W. G. *Values in the Comprehensive School*. Similar reports have appeared in *Forum*.

changes. They blur the outlines of analysis and discussion, yet lie one degree nearer the sources of our problems.

Two points can be made about the teachers who came into these enquiries. Firstly, very few of them had much knowledge about teaching methods, school organization, or the possibilities of education outside the system which prevailed in their present school or the school they attended in childhood. Most seemed to think that some method of early selection was universal—an original fact of life, rather than an artifact of British life. This was typified by teachers who said that an unstreamed class or school would be: 'Impossible' 'Chaotic' 'The height of professional irresponsibility'. These comments are not only hostile to non-streaming. They are often ignorant of it as a *fact* in some British schools and in almost all similar schools in other industrial societies. Viewed internationally, it is the 'streamed' teachers who are the minority; and whether their decisions are right or wrong, the 'closed' nature of their knowledge is in itself disturbing.

Secondly, teachers' beliefs were largely beliefs in very limited ability, and in distinct 'kinds' of children. Most teachers assumed the extreme scarceness of talent ('cream, train and cream again'). This was so even in a school like Honey Bell. And in less dynamic schools the values were naked: behind the speech-day talk of all children being treated in accordance with their needs, were the crude facts of 'C' classes in the poorest accommodation, of 'C' teachers being less qualified, less promoted, less well-paid. And yet, these very 'C' stream teachers were also the staunchest defenders of the *status quo*. They were an image of the enclosed nature of the teaching profession—locked in the systems of their childhood, imprisoned within the values of one type of school. One of the clearest needs in schools was for much more movement, visiting, reading, experimenting, reflection by the staff. Without a freer play of mind amongst the teachers, there will always be the hazard of confined, predetermined or deflected growth amongst the children.

How does the rest of the world manage?

It helps to see what happens in other countries, similar to our own. In the United States, or nations like Canada, New Zealand or Australia there is nothing comparable to our streaming of primary children. All these 'new frontier' societies have educational systems that are more democratic, less hierarchical. Children are usually promoted on the 'grade placement' system, whereby the teacher's aim must be to help *all* children reach the next academic level—and then move them, as a group, up to the next class. Clearly this produces a quite different emphasis from our own, and whereas it doesn't seem to breed so many dull children, critics will obviously want to know what happens to the gifted child. Even if they are satisfied by the sheer wealth of very able boys and girls in the United States, they will want to know if there is any 'concealed' streaming. The problem of excellence in a more 'open' system of this type is a real one; and I suspect that in some parts of America, there *are* 'concealed' forms of streaming at work. But without venturing further, it quite alters our focus on English education if we see the 'new frontier' societies apparently flourishing, without thrusting so many of their energies into the hunt of the future elite.

The older European countries are of course more hierarchical in their educational ideas. The only one near to the United States in spirit here is the U.S.S.R., where streaming was abolished in 1936; from that date there has been a huge upsurge of talented children, though all that can hardly be credited to unstreaming. Slightly nearer to us are the Scandinavian countries, which have known streaming in the past but are now abandoning it. In Norway it is illegal. In Denmark it is impossible at the primary school stage, and at the secondary school stage they are trying a system whereby parents at each school are balloted, and decide themselves whether they want a form of streaming or not. In Sweden the change from a 'closed' to an 'open' system has largely been based on, or accompanied by considerable research. For example, a large amount of action research was possible when the city of Stockholm was divided in half. One part had comprehensive schooling, one part had a form of divided secondary schooling similar to our own. Academic progress of matched groups in both halves were compared, and—to summarise crudely—the backward children were much fewer and more successful under the 'open' system; the average child also fared much better, and there was little to choose between either system as far as the academic scores at the top were concerned.[1] Sweden has never had severe forms of early selection, like our own primary school streaming. But this secondary school experiment looks similar to the patches of research we have on academic differences between streamed and unstreamed primary schools.

In other European countries such as France, Germany, Belgium, Holland and Italy the educational system is infused by a system of hierarchical values not so dissimilar to our own. In none is there anything close to our primary school streaming, though I suspect there must sometimes be 'concealed' streaming. Our organization of children's education between 5 years and 11 years, is an extreme practice—and every year our position becomes more isolated, more questioned by research. Oddly, the country sometimes nearest to us is South Africa, where the most severe forms of segregation are being developed. It separates white and black children; and not only puts them in different schools but on a different syllabus so as to create different levels of expectation (farm labour is sometimes regarded as an integral part of the black child's school education). It is a caricature of our 'A' and 'C' streaming. And at the secondary level where, as in the Transvaal, there is a tight three stream system even for white pupils, some official statements are the nearest I can find to extreme remarks made in this country by the supporters of the streaming principle. The Transvaal Director of Education, for example, is on record as opposing fluid transfer from stream to stream:

> 'In the choice of courses every child should be treated with the greatest consideration and respect for personality. Children should not be shifted about like so many pawns on the chessboard.'

He catches both the speech-day flavour of the English school ('greatest consideration and respect') together with the rigidity revealed ('not be shifted about') when the school records are examined.

In England, streaming is the norm and deliberate unstreaming is uncommon. In substance this, as most of the material documented here, applies to Wales and Scotland too; their

---

[1] See Svensson, N. E., 'Ability Grouping and Scholastic Achievement' in *Educational Research,* November, 1962, and Husen, T., 'Educational Structure and the Development of Ability' in Halsey, A. H., *Ability and Educational Opportunity.*

differences, though real, are the local differences of a small island, coloured-up by national tradition. But if we look outwards to other societies the position is reversed. The English drive for early selection is abnormal, and the unstreamed principle is generally followed by the civilized world in the education of young children.

Some proposals on primary school streaming

Primary school streaming has such far-spreading roots that I doubt if any proposals I can raise would help us see whether it is England or the rest of the world that is out of step—or whether different steps should be followed in different societies. Further research is needed, but not only into academic results of streaming. This is already under way, and it is both clear to see its importance and relatively less difficult to persuade Government bodies or the great Trusts to finance it. But much more research is needed into the values and pressures behind selection in our schools, both primary and secondary. Such research is difficult, and results—since they play on social values—will always arouse controversy. But many of the important lines run this way: and if we are to know ourselves as we really are, even small scale probes, risking 'subjectivity', may drag back results out of all proportion to the size of the venture. A central plea here is not only the need for more research, but for the support of research which goes beyond the present boundaries of the measurable, accepting the attendant losses but searching for those insights which re-illuminate knowledge.

Only huge changes in our society, and an end to selection for secondary education will make much difference to streaming. But there are three small proposals I would like to raise here, not designed to 'abolish' streaming, but to allow teachers to make more informed choices:

1. *More mobile teachers.* There is a great need for teachers to escape from their own classrooms and schools, to see other systems in action, to discuss and reflect on what they are doing. Neither of the two proposals below can be new, but neither are vigorously pursued as yet:

Time away. Every teacher should spend at least one week of each year visiting and observing in other schools. This needs to be seen as an obligatory and essential part of his *work*, not a fringe relaxation. Local teacher shortages should not over-rule it. It is better for all if the teacher has a week away like this, even if it means that his own class is given extra sport instead of lessons, or simply allowed half days off. The work-aday administrative problem should take second place to the general principle.

Training Head Teachers. At the moment Heads of schools receive no special training to fit them for their post. From time to time courses for Heads are available, but no serious or obligatory training. I suggest the creation of regular train-ing courses for Headteachers (even a month would be valu-able) in which strong emphasis is again placed on visiting schools, on watching (perhaps through closed circuit tele-vision) different classes and different techniques. The Head must be placed in a position where he sees himself making *choices*—of organization, of technique, of content. And then he must be given some advice on how to execute his choice—so that, for example, he does not choose to unstream and then disrupt his school by tackling it the wrong way. Much more could be given to Heads than this (especially some help on the secretarial side of school administration, since many Heads conduct this with methods and equipment 50 years out of date). But the prime aim should again be to release them from the constricting side of their own experience.

2. *Teachers in Training*. Teacher training colleges already bear so many responsibilities, and are so badly treated as 'outside' or 'junior' bodies to our university system, that it is hard to suggest they should do more. Subjects such as educational sociology are likely to be left to the odd extra period or considered covered by an occasional visiting lecturer. At the time of writing I have only been able to discover two sociology lecturers amongst the 3,980 who are currently teaching in 124 colleges. There may be others, but clearly they are an infinitesimal proportion. Even allowing for what their colleagues in other subjects must inevit-ably touch upon, few of the questions raised by this book can be receiving sustained attention from those who most need to give it. So the unbroken circle revolves. It is always hard to establish a new subject without special help. There is a case here for a

special increase in training college budgets to allow them to take on sociology lecturers. In competition with the universities they will not be easy to find. (They could often be *shared* with a university). But as a 'starter', extra finance might be allocated to, say, 12 training colleges in the North of England (where traditional patterns are less questioned). This might well be enough to start this advance, and would cost less than £20,000 a year: a small price.

3. *An Experimental Branch.* The above proposals are modest in scale, and before leaving this I want to sketch out a further idea which would act as a device against our educational system hardening and closing up.

Advance in English education is usually made by individuals working alone against the accepted patterns around them. It is the rare Director of Education who creates a new school system, it is the isolated 'C' stream teacher who makes discoveries about the use of music in the classroom. But experiment and advance can, to some extent, be built into a school system. This happened with the 'progressive' private schools between the wars. They had parents who chose to send children there, they had the confidence that some of their discoveries were paying off. They were an informal institution for experimental education from which the state system drew benefit.

This enquiry into primary school streaming suggests to me the need for an 'experimental' branch in the State system. A number of primary and secondary schools might be responsible directly to the Ministry instead of local education authorities. These schools could be staffed by 'advanced' teachers: men and women who had successfully attended a special Ministry course. There would be no doubt of their talents and competence. In schools in the experimental branch they would take part in the use of new techniques—whether mechanical aids such as teaching machines, or creative methods such as 'free writing'. Some schools might place the stress here, others might be especially concerned with new approaches to discipline or organization. These would be schools working at the frontier of education, despatching news of fresh discoveries to the centre. This 'despatch' would be helped if the experimental schools were so staffed that there was adequate time for their teachers to write accounts of their work or sometimes be sent 'on tour' giving demonstration lessons. It would also be helpful if the experimental branch was not confined to a group of schools, but 'owned' single classrooms in ordinary schools, so that the systems dovetailed. Schools of this kind would have to be situated so that parents could *choose* to send a child there or not: a basis as essential for them as it was to Dartington Hall or Summerhill. Some of the advances tried certainly ought to involve the parents.

The problem of streaming is a problem of the surface when compared to the ever-hardening attitudes behind it. An academic system—like the huge scholastic system of Mandarin China—can grow vaster and more complex—whilst education itself is in full retreat.

8

EPILOGUE: CHILDREN OF GOLD

B Y the year 380 B.C. Plato, experimenting with the notion of an ideal society had invented the 'magnificent myth'. Socrates in *The Republic* explains to Glaucon:

'We shall', I said, 'address our citizens as follows:

"You are, all of you in this land, brothers. But when God fashioned you, he added gold in the composition of those of you who are qualified to be Rulers (which is why their prestige is greatest); he put silver in the Auxiliaries, and iron and bronze in the farmers and the rest. Now since you are all of the same stock, though children will commonly resemble their parents, occasionally a silver child will be born of golden parents, or a golden child of silver parents, and so on. Therefore the first and most important of God's commandments to the Rulers is that they must exercise their function as Guardians with particular care in watching the mixture of metals in the characters of the children. If one of their own children has bronze or iron in its make-up, they must harden their hearts, and degrade it to the ranks of the industrial and agricultural class where it properly belongs: similarly, if a child of this class is born with gold or silver in its nature, they will promote it appropriately to be a Guardian or an Auxiliary. For they know that there is a prophecy that the State will be ruined when it has Guardians of silver or bronze." That is the story. Do you think there is any way of making them believe it?'

'Not in the first generation,' he said, 'but you might succeed with the second and later generations.'[1]

Glaucon was right. The 'magnificent myth' has survived uncommonly well. Plato imagines three broad classes of people— the gold, the silver, the baser metals. He stresses inherited

[1] *The Republic* trans. H. D. P. Lee, Penguin, 1955.

ability: 'born with gold or silver in its nature'—yet is concerned to bring it out and purify it by the appropriate education, for even gold can be lost or obscured. And he associates human excellence not with the metals of more immediate use—iron, bronze—but with the metals that are limited and scarce—gold, then silver. With considerable effort and a trained eye, man can prospect. But he cannot create them. So with the children of gold: they are to be discovered not made. Not even the finest silver can be transmuted into the premier metal.

I suppose the three-fold division has magical origins. Certainly it has a magical persistence in our thinking. It would be absurd to press the point too strongly: other numbers also have their natural persistence. But an older generation usually accepted that our grandparents' society (like its railway carriages) had its 1st, 2nd, and 3rd class: upper, middle and lower. Our world combines this ironic echo. In school uniform the child learns of the teacher—prefect—pupil triad. In army uniform he meets the firmness of the officer—NCO—men structure. The BBC 'naturally' postulates three audiences, Third—Home—Light. And so our secondary school system—like Plato's — is tripartite[1]: grammar — technical — secondary modern. Education is tripartite at other points too and especially so in the ABC of streaming. Even the most sober educational statements display the ancient magic. For example, at the end of that very fine and scrupulous report *Half Our Future,* after listening to the evidence of many witnesses and reporting the statistics of special surveys, the committee make one recommendation on streaming for the pupils they are concerned with:

'Excessively fine grading of ability groups should be avoided; more than three broad groupings is probably unnecessary, and

---

[1] In the *Guardian* of November 22nd, 1961, a correspondent reported that outside Marple Grammar School, Cheshire stood an expensive signboard, which read:

Cheshire County Council

Headmaster:
Reginald Hill, M.A., Cantab.,

Clerk to the Governors:
E. Richards, Esq.

Caretaker: H. Hewitt.

groupings in the final years at school should be largely based on subject or course choices.[1]

But of course. This is exactly what all the teachers favouring streaming would have said. Those who felt that children's brains were like eggs—large, medium and small—would not demur at this. Nor would the teachers in 5 stream, 7 stream or 9 stream junior schools. Even though they divided their pupils into 'E' streams or 'G' streams, they thought essentially in terms of *three real divisions* of which 'E' or 'G' were merely administrative sub-sections. One six-stream school, for example, called its classes A1, A2; B1, B2; C1, C2. The Newsom triad is familiar. And when we search through that report—asking why not two groups? or four broad groups? or none at all?— we are, despite the statistics, the visiting and the long committee hours, given no evidence. It is as if none were needed or expected. We are back at the magical roots.

Behind Plato's myth of the metals lie a tenacious cluster of assumptions that it will be hard to remove from English education over 2,000 years later. People are thought of as single *units*—this one has gold, that one has not. Yet they are also treated as *types*—the golden ones, the base metal groups. They are unchanging creatures, their potentiality alters little: not gold one day, iron the next—or gold from this angle but silver from that. And they belong to a world of scarcity—all metals are valuable, but gold is the most valuable and the rarest. In a rough and ready way the old assumptions still persist.

No doubt the system in which we embed them is nothing like so severe as the one Plato considered ('If one of their own children has bronze or iron in its make-up, they must harden their hearts, and degrade it to the ranks of the industrial and agricultural class . . .'). With us the stress on original gold merges into our sense of inherited ability and early training, so that our golden ones have mastered the art of passing on their golden touch. The question of 'degrading' *their* children hardly arises. In the state system of education the results can be crudely summarized as shown in table 39.

We take 100 children and divide them up into those from manual workers' homes ('working class') and those from non-

---

[1] *Half our Future.* H.M.S.O., 1963. p.xvi.

TABLE 39

PROGRESS OF 100 CHILDREN THROUGH STATE SCHOOLS

	At Birth	In the 'A' stream at 7	Passing 11 plus	Still being educated at 18
Middle Class Children	25	15	12	7
Working Class Children	75	24	12	3
Total	100	39	24	10

manual homes ('middle class'), and send them to a three stream primary school. At the age of seven, 39 have been pre-selected: the social balance of their school class is quite different from that of the community as a whole. At eleven, 24 of these go on to selective education. The first forms of their new school have yet another composition—half and half, whereas the community is dominantly one of manual workers. By the age of 18, the numbers have dropped again and the balance tipped quite the other way. The table reminds us that there *is* a problem here, and that in some sense it is certainly a problem of class. And further that there are three points where the children of iron are put aside or withdraw—through streaming in the primary school, through selection for secondary education, and by exit after the school leaving age.

But these 'children of iron' are no such thing. Some are extremely talented in exactly the way in which talent is measured and prized within the system. The National Foundation for Educational Research reports that under the best 11 plus selection techniques we know, there is still an 'irreducible error' of 10 per cent. That is to say that if there were a clear grammar school/secondary modern division after 11 throughout the country, each year about 70,000 children would arrive at the 'wrong' school.[1] The Crowther Committee in their 1959 report.[2]

[1] The Foundation usefully summarises evidence on the accuracy of selection in *Procedures for the Allocation of Pupils in Secondary Education.* (N.F.E.R. 1963).

[2] *15-18*, H.M.S.O., 1959.

divided a sample of 5,940 military recruits into groups according to their scores in a battery. In the group which contained the top tenth, 42 per cent. had left school by 16. Professor Kelsall, analyzing in 1963[1] the latest available figures, pointed out once again how children coming from working class homes still fail to realise the expectations raised by their scores at 11 plus. The situation in which children had roughly equal chances 'demonstrably does not exist, and would not appear to have come materially nearer existing'. The Robbins Report of 1963 added to the story. So they continue.

All these are measurements of golden children missed *within the terms of the system as it stands*. But if instead of assessing children on tests examining the speed and accuracy of their logical faculties, we divided children according to their scores on a 'creative' intelligence test,[2] where what counted was enterprising, divergent thought, no doubt the gold and iron would be more confused. And if we did none of this, but defined human excellence in items of imagination, sympathy, tenacity, courage, as well as rational speed, then the present structure looks capable of limiting the spread of excellence in its hunt for isolated nuggets of gold.

Our society is one of opportunity and possible plenty. We reduce its potentialities by an educational sieve designed for a society of scarcity. In the past the sieve served well enough. It could be argued that when society's resources were more limited, it was sensible to pioneer the way forward by concentrating on the education of a small band of pupils. Streaming is a means to this end. But our society has changed. Our children are not whipped into 'compulsory' school. Rather the reverse. Parents demand more provision than the state makes. Education is desired, not resented. And if we so choose, our society can pay for it as the inter-war society could not. Yet whether we

[1] Getting on at the Grammar' by Kelsall, R. K., *Times Educational Supplement*, March 15th, 1963.

[2] See Jackson, P. W. and Getzels, J. W. *Creativity and Intelligence*. An introduction to work by Hudson, L. on similar lines in this country can be found in *Where? 14*. There is an excellent critical review of Jackson and Getzels by Burt, C., in the *British Journal of Educational Psychology*, vol. xxxii, part 3, 1962.

will it or not, our chances of a huge *qualitative* advance in education are frustrated by a system which pushes aside the child reared in unfortunate or unvalued circumstances. Both the child who comes through and the child who is put aside suffer. I have not, in this study, considered the disadvantages of being an 'A' stream child, but I think they are real enough.

Consider some of the *overlapping* categories which contain the children of iron.

1. The manual workers' children. Note: Of manual workers' sons reaching 11 between 1931-40, only 1.7 per cent. reached university (for white collar workers it was 8.5 per cent.). Of manual workers' sons reaching 11 between 1946-51, only 1.6 per cent. reached university (for white collar workers it was 19.2 per cent.).[1] Change comes very slowly.

2. Family size. Note: The larger the family—whatever its social standing—the less likely are the children to successfully pass the selection sieves. Only children, or the first-born child of two tend to pass the 11 plus,[2] children from larger families score less well in IQ tests, and leave school earlier.[3] Just possibly the order of birth within a family counts in our system.[4] Brothers and sisters are an educational handicap.

3. Town or country. Like the other categories this overlaps with class (especially migration from the countryside) and varying local provision. But country children do less well on selection tests not only for reasons of class, provision or migration—but also because our selection system is designed to match an urban

---

[1] Floud, J., 'Social Class Factors in Educational Achievement' in Halsey, A. M., Flood, J., and Anderson, C. A., *Education, Economy and Society.*

[2] See Stewart, M., *The Success of the First Born Child*, 1962, and Douglas, J. W. B., *The Home and the School* (1964).

[3] See *15-18* p. 119.

[4] See *The Success of the First Born Child* above; also 'Environmental Conditions Affecting Intelligence' by Lynn, R. in *Educational Research* Vol. 1. No. 3., June, 1959 and 'Family or Sibship Position and Scholastic Ability' by Lees, J.P. and Stewart, A. H. in *Sociological Review* Vol. 5. Nos. 1 and 2. Yet neither the Crowther nor Robbins reports throw light on this: the evidence is inconclusive, the mystery remains. But as Douglas, J. W. B. shows in *The Home and The School* (pps. 98-100) the whole question of family size and intelligence, once confidently explained in terms of 'hereditary' factors, is more and more being mapped out as an 'environmental' problem.

ideology. Note: Verbal selection tests are tests of urban vocabulary. What city child would spot the misfit here—stirk, gilt, reckling, hoggett, colt?[1]

4. Nervous or troubled children sink scholastically, and then in our "streamed' system readjust themselves to lower goals. Note: At each level of measured ability children with nervous symptoms are less likely to pass through selection nets. 'The extent of their disadvantage may be summarized by saying that they get 10 per cent. fewer places than expected *after taking their measured ability into account,* whereas children with few reported symptoms get 2 per cent. more places?[2] Physically, children who pass our early selection tests tend to be taller and stronger too. Streaming handicaps the handicapped.

5. Birthday or bad luck. Chapter two suggests that matters as fortuitous as date of birth can affect a child's chances. So do more obviously unfortunate circumstances such as losing a parent, having an unemployed or disabled father. Even left handedness is associated with the handicapped group.

The above are not distinct categories. Often an unlucky child falls into several. But they serve to give a sense of the kind of child who is tested as gold or iron by the huge selection machine that we have built. The machine has its own law. Two code words summarize it: if a child has SUPREMO he is likely to be gold. If he is found to be WORSWUN the system gives him little chance.

Strong	Weaker build
Urban	Other children in family
Parents educated	Rural
Right birthday	Summer-born
Emotionally stable	Working class
Middle class	Unstable home
Only child	Nervous

[1] Mentioned by Semmens, H. in 'Rural Reorganization' in the *Journal of Education* Vol. 90., March, 1958, and quoted in 'Urban and Rural Differences in Ability and Attainment' by Barr, F., in *Educational Research* Vol. 1. No. 2.

[2] See 'Emotional Adjustment and Educational Achievement' by Douglas, J. W. B. and Mulligan, D. G. in *Proceedings of the Royal Society of Medicine,* Vol. 54, No. 10, October, 1961, pps. 885-891.

Children of Gold

Last voices

Selection is imperfect, original inequalities of circumstance take a heavy toll, the gifted child is not always perceived and consequently is lost: stress and anxiety may be frequent. All this can be defended. A distinguished advocate, Sir Cyril Burt, argues that:

> 'After all every one of us, however successful, has sooner or later to acknowledge that there are others better than we are. And it should be an essential part of the child's education to teach him how to face a possible beating in the 11 plus or any other examination, just as he should learn to take a beating in a half-mile race, or in a bout with boxing gloves or a football match with a rival school.'[1]

The comparisons ('take a beating in a half-mile race') are as illuminating as the statements. This is the world of the public school élite, not of England today. There is a point at which we step beyond objective science and assert our values, at which we all 'read' the same evidence differently. The values that associate early selection with defeat on the playing fields are real enough: many teachers and parents share them—and in the world between 1850 and 1950 they were extraordinarily effective. There was no *economic* point in raising large hopes through education, for society had not the resources to satisfy them. Early selection of the few allowed the governing élites to recruit a new stream of talent from lower middle class homes. Eleven plus and streaming clarified the problem. It was as objective as any such procedures. It worked.

Before 1939 early selection made some sense. It was not just, but it was the nearest to justice that circumstance allowed. Today it is absurd. It limits us, occupying our attention with the tiny details that divide and label us—drawing energies away from the colossal opportunities for human development that our wealth and knowledge promise.

'At school we didn't think about class as such, not in any open or sophisticated way. But all the same it bit into you every day. When I was 13 or so—getting into puberty—I felt it intensely in the boys' showers. All the boys would strip off, and then the

[1] 'The Examination at Eleven Plus' by Sir Cyril Burt in *British Journal of Educational Studies,* Vol. 7, No. 2, pp. 99-118.

141

K

difference showed. Almost all the middle-class kids in the school had been circumcised as infants, whereas what working class kids there were at that school, hadn't. Of course it was all a joke. They looked at their penises and called them Roundheads, and pointed at ours and called them Cavaliers. It was all a joke, but a joke I cared about bitterly, I wished to God I was middle class and circumcised—and a Roundhead too.

Years afterwards when I left school, I joined the army and was posted to Suez. They put a notice up that men who wished to, could be circumcised: feasible enough because all the grit and sand and dirt was likely to get up your penis. I was about the first to volunteer. It was 50% for medical reasons, but 50% for the old Roundheads and Cavaliers. I remember thinking: thank God, now that's done with. For kids like me it was a fight to come through. It was much easier for the Cavaliers—the school was designed for them.

The last thing I want is for *my* children to face school like a battlefield.'

Our next step is to end all early selection. Disguising it, by substituting teachers' estimates and moves of that sort, is a backward step. If there is no division of roads at $11+$, $12+$ or $13+$, then selection at seven may also disappear. The proposals in the previous section are aimed at that end. But even if streaming itself formally disappears and if the comprehensive principle replaces the selection principle, the problems touched on here will not vanish. Teachers' attitudes are slower to change, and so long as they believe and think about types of children, *there will be* types of children. Streaming goes deep, and in some form it is likely to be our concern for many years to come. The proposals raised may do something to help. Much more must be done by the finest creative teaching, exploiting the resources of language, drama, music, art. Such teaching will enhance our respect for the complexity of children, the many-sidedness of human gifts. Perhaps this overstates the case. For clearly there are at this time still gaps in the evidence on which it must rest. And school and all its doings are only a section of a child's life, touch only a part of its personality.

But we know enough to know we are wrong. We have built a system which has served its purpose. It changes on the surface, very little underneath. It still assumes and searches for the children of gold, whereas human excellence is more subtle and diverse. Excellence may have genetic limits, but we must alter circumstance a great deal before the genes finally stop our growth. Meanwhile our colossal technical resources can serve an imaginative approach to education, and rediscover what every great civilization of the past stumbled on. In favourable circumstances, excellence is not static or severely limited. It multiplies.

APPENDIX 1

The Home and the School

IN my previous chapters I report the state of affairs as it was in 1962 (Chapters 2-5) and 1963 (Chapter 6). In these chapters the children discussed are usually either 7 or 11 years old. They were therefore born between 1951 and 1955 (Chapters 2-5) or 1952 and 1956 (Chapter 6).

The practice and frequency of streaming must be changing, and I would expect that the last two years have seen an increase in the number of unstreamed primary schools. But change may come more slowly than we realise, as I was reminded when J. W. B. Douglas' book *The Home and the School* (McGibbon & Kee, 1964) was published shortly after I had completed my own last chapter.

Dr. Douglas' fascinating study is part of the series[1] reporting on a sample of 5,362 children born during the first week of March 1946. *The Home and The School* chiefly considers the progress of his sample through primary school, and its information largely concerns how the children fared between 1954 and 1959, when they were aged 8 to 11 years. It therefore reports the situation as it was some 3 to 9 years before the scene I have tried to sketch. It does so with a statistical magnificence quite beyond my resources or my ability.

Chapter 14 of *The Home and The School* concerns primary school streaming. 491 children on Dr. Douglas' sample attended 2 stream primary schools; 62 per cent. were in the 'A' stream and 38 per cent. in the 'B' stream. It was rare for these children to change streams; over the whole three year period the annual rate of transfer was 2.3 per cent. Between the ages of 8 and 11, the 'A' stream children improved their test scores by 0.71 points, and the 'B' stream children deteriorated by 0.49 points. In the 'A' classes the spread of test scores was 17 per cent. less at 11 years than at 8 years, but unchanged in the 'B' streams. So bright children in 'B' streams gradually got poorer, weak children in 'A' streams improved and the gap opened between 'A' and 'B'. It is noticeable that it was the weak or

---

[1] The first two books are Douglas, J. W. B. and Rowntree, G., *Maternity in Great Britain* (1948), and Douglas, J. W. B. and Bloomfield, J. M., *Children under Five* (1958).

average 'A' stream child who strongly pushed his score up, the children at the top of the 'A' stream did not improve so very much.

On Dr. Douglas' sample there were 11 per cent. more middle class children in 'A' streams than would be expected from their measured ability, and 26 per cent. fewer in the 'B' streams. In the 'A' streams both middle and working class children improved their scores, though the middle class children went up 3 to 4 times as much as the others. In the 'B' streams the middle class child still improved, though only half as much as if he had been in an 'A' stream; but the working class child deteriorated severely. Being in a low stream was a handicap, but it was a much bigger handicap to a working class child than anyone else. A working class child in a 'B' stream was—in these terms—duller when the school had finished with him at 11 years than he was when his parents handed him over at 5 years.

It is unlikely that we will ever get a better statistical record of how the self-fulfilling prophecy works. Dr. Douglas speculates very little on the implications of his impressive evidence. But it looks as if he has arithmetically sketched the way in which society's dominant group knits the schools into standards and values so as to produce a school system which strongly favours its own children whilst appearances of justice and equality are suitably preserved.

APPENDIX 2

A BRIEF HISTORY OF STREAMING

STREAMING is more familiar to our children than to us. Consider the techniques it has replaced. Young children in Victorian schools were grouped by 'Standards'. A simple examination or 'Standard' was set in reading, writing and arithmetic, and those who passed it were all placed together in Standard I.[1] Here they prepared for a more difficult 'standard' and those who passed this were moved into Standard II, and so on. Children of similar achievement but differing ages made up one class.

The teacher's income varied according to the number of boys and girls he coached through to the next Standard. It was payment by results. Consequently there was a financial interest tempting the teacher to concentrate on the *average* child, and thrust as many of them as he possibly could through the examination. The very bright child, certain to succeed to the next Standard, could be left to look after himself; and there was every chance to neglect altogether the very weakest children, for teaching whom there was little chance of being paid. Nor was it clear that the weakest children of all *could* profitably be attended to. Perhaps their condition was the unchangeable and unchallengeable 'will of God'.

Towards the end of the century the mood changed. After 1895 'payment by results' faded out, to linger as a faintly menacing shadow in the minds of older teachers. In 1899 the school-leaving age was raised to 12, and ambitious headteachers, despite the hostile intervention of the authorities[2], began to design 'secondary school' courses for their older and abler pupils. At the beginning of this century the outlines of the education system were fairly clear,

[1] The test for Standard 1 was 'to read narrative jn monosyllables . . . to form on blackboard or slate from dictation, letters, capital and small manuscript, to form similarly from dictation figures up to 20, to name at sight figures up to 20, to add and subtract figures up to 10 orally from examples of blackboard.' See Dent, H. C., *Secondary Education for All*.

[2] Headteachers were warned, for example, not to intrude into 'grammar school work'. For an account of the impulse for secondary education 'from below', and the hostility it sometimes met with 'from above', see Dent, H. C., *Secondary Education For All*.

though the relative importance of the various parts was not. Primary education for all was partly achieved. Some abler boys and girls were passing on from primary schools to a developing network of what might be called secondary schools with a technical bias—the 'Higher Grade School', and the 'Junior Technical'. Here practical skills and scientific training flourished alongside the traditional academic syllabus. Meanwhile the exclusively bookish line of learning, centred in the study of Greek and Latin, was the prerogative of the old-established Grammar Schools. But the grammar schools were generally impoverished and frail and it was not at all obvious what their connections were with the needs of the new century. And behind all these were the public schools of the upper middle class—buoyant, various and prosperous.

As pressure for more secondary education intensified from the schools, and as the worlds of business and industry demanded better trained boys and girls ('or else we'll import clerks from Germany'), the decisive question was: What should the state secondary school be like? Should it be, like the old Grammar School, a place of Greek, Latin and related disciplines for the very few?[1] Or should it be based on the higher grade school, allowing for greater diversity of talent in a larger number of pupils and recognising the scientific and technological present: a place for metal work, thermodynamics, and draughtsmanship, as well as classical studies?

If one man took the decision for the nation it was Robert Morant. Morant was an ex-public school boy, educated at the most academic of English public schools—Winchester. He returned from a post as tutor to the Prince of Siam to one in the Board of Education, intensely desiring that the education system of the twentieth century should be modelled on schools like his own.[2] This would mean repairing and adding to the old Grammar School foundations, fitting them for the present age as the keystone to a new system. It would also mean rubbing out the challenge of the Higher Grade School. Morant took home the evidence given to a government commission,

[1] The number of children then considered suitable for a grammar school education was about 1 per cent. (After the dissolution of the monasteries in 1546 the figure was probably close to 0.5 per cent.). At the present moment it is almost as low as 10 per cent. in some parts of England, and nearly 40 per cent. in some parts of Wales.

[2] 'A convinced adherent to the classical and literary tradition of secondary education' he 'saw in the Higher Grade School an insuperable obstacle to the only kind of secondary education he was capable of imagining.' Dent, H. C., *Secondary Education For All*, p. 28. Both Dent and Lowndes, G. A. N., *The Silent Social Revolution* (from whom the supposition about answer 35,481 comes) tell the story well, and catch its social typicality.

and probing through it, phrase by phrase, tumbled on answer 35,481 and its implications, which had escaped lawyers, councillors and Parliament. The Higher Grade Schools were illegal. According to the strict letter of the law a local council had no right to pay for them out of the rates. A test case followed, and the illegality was confirmed. Morant had his way, and when the state's secondary system was established with the Education Act of 1902, it centred on the revivified Grammar School.

After 1902, with more grammar schools being built, there was increasing pressure on the primary schools to promote their brightest pupils to 'free places'. Primary school teachers consequently organised their classes in such a way that the obviously gifted child could move rapidly into the top class, whilst the obviously dull child remained in the bottom classes. The top classrooms might contain extremely able children of eight sitting alongside average girls of ten, and very backward boys waiting for their twelfth birthday. Such a system overrode the differences in emotional needs, and indeed physical needs, classifying children according to their level of academic attainment. In the old 'payment by results' system the characteristic class had consisted of the central group of *average* children advancing in a body, standard by standard; in the new system the moving life of the school was the small group of *very able* children rising rapidly through the school in search of the grammar school 'free place'.

Problems concealed by the school system were freshly seen as the work of Binet on 'intelligence', and then, after the 1914-18 war, Burt's research into 'backwardness' spread through the schools. It became possible to classify children more neatly. In the Hadow Report of 1926[1], which urged that the nineteenth century achievement of primary education for all should now be followed by a twentieth century attempt at secondary schooling for all, we see the first plea for the 'sectional treatment' of children. Boys and girls are to be divided, whenever possible, into able, average, and backward groups. 'Streaming' has arrived.

Five years later in the highly influential *Report on the Primary School*[2], streaming is most strongly urged, as being the best way of

1 *The Education of the Adolescent,* Report of the Consultative Committee, 1926.

2 'The break at the age of eleven has rendered possible a more thorough classification of children. It is important that this opportunity should be turned to the fullest account . . . in very large primary schools there might, wherever possible, be a triple track system of organisation, viz. a series of "A" classes or groups for the bright children, and a series of

turning any break between primary and secondary school at eleven 'to the fullest account'. And in the *1937 Handbook for Teachers*[1] it is assumed to be highly desirable. The spread of streaming in the 1930's was still limited; for only a very small minority of schools were large enough to have two or three classrooms for each year group of children. But nevertheless two distinct results followed: Firstly, very bright boys and girls moved forward as a highly teachable year group, no longer scattered amongst older children, regardless of physical and emotional growth. Secondly, the new 'B' and 'C' classes threw into illuminating prominence the huge problem of backwardness in the schools—bigger by far than many capable teachers had realised. And before long small numbers of gifted and dedicated teachers were choosing to work with such classes, developing new techniques for teaching the weaker child, pushing back the frontiers of ignorance and piercing the deeper kinds of emotional blockage.

The war of 1939-45 changed even streaming. Queues and rationing sharpening men's sense of equality: evacuees, air-raids, long years in the barrack rooms, and fighting itself drew remote social classes into shared experience. The new spirit of 'togetherness' in society was felt in the schools. And in the final years, as victory became promise and then reality, it was natural that hopes should turn to children, to schools and to more education for everyone. The 1944 Education Act offered a secondary education to every child, and made the break at 11 more of a physical reality than it had been.[2] The glass-and-concrete of new school building became an increasingly common sight.

The consequences for children in 'A', 'B' or 'C' classes were somewhat ironical. On the one hand official reports became increasingly uneasy about the idea of children being streamed at all; largely, I think, because Inspectors saw so much cramming in 'A' classes and so much coarse teaching in 'C' classes. The 1945 *The Nation's Schools*[3] wonders uncertainly if 'grading on this basis may in future

---

[1] *Handbook of Suggestions for Teachers.* Board of Education, H.M.S.O., 1937.

[2] Though even in 1960 there were still more all-age schools (1,281) than grammar schools (1,268) in England and Wales.

[3] *The Nation's Schools.* Ministry of Education Pamphlet No. 1.

"C" classes or groups to include retarded children, both series being parallel to the ordinary series of "B" classes.'

not appear so desirable as it does now.' And by 1959 *Primary Education*[1] is so uninvolved that it sees streaming as a principle 'peculiar to our own day', and tactfully advises teachers that it is also possible to work profitably with normal classes of boys and girls in which all kinds and talents are mixed together.[2]

The magnificent new building programmes meant that more and more children were being educated in separate primary schools. Since the primary school was four years smaller in age range than the all-age school, it could usually manage to accept more classes to a year than previously. So when senior children left for glass palaces in the suburbs, and tiny city schools closed down completely, primary school heads with several classes to each year had an *increased* opportunity to stream their pupils.

At the same time, the newly-built were usually large and suitable for two, three or four classes per year: the head teacher was compelled to stand by some principle in grouping his children, and again the opportunity to stream was increased. In most teachers' eyes streaming had been a tried and proved method, and despite the uneasiness of officialdom, head teachers took their opportunities, and primary school streaming appears to have spread with barely credible rapidity all over the country since 1945.

We might summarise by saying that the history of state education shows that the first problem was to give primary education of a narrowly practical kind to all, and then secondary education of different kinds. Education improves, schools become more plentiful, teachers more skilled and children come more readily and naturally to class than they did in the days when Attendance Officer, 'School Board Man' or 'Whipper In' patrolled the streets. But the 'class' that children attend has itself changed considerably. The Victorian class was usually confined to one sex, and under the payment by results system it had a wide spread of ages, but a narrow spread of attainment. George may be six and Mary eleven, but both read in

[1] *Primary Education,* H.M.S.O., 1959.

[2] 'One of the most remarkable developments in teachers' skill over the last decade or so has been that of educating in one class children of very different abilities. They do this by arranging the environment in the classroom and school so that the children learn a great deal for themselves, either individually or in small groups. The teacher comes to know when to teach groups and when to teach the class or an individual, and in time he knows at what pace and in what ways the different groups of children learn best. To acquire this are is no mean achievement, though to many who have an understanding of children and a fertile inventiveness it appears to come easily. Others proceed more slowly, learning as they go, and are wise to avoid arrangements too ambitious or too complicated for their capacity.' *Primary Education,* H.M.S.O., 1959, p. 70.

monosyllables and so sit side by side. Then very gradually the sex barrier broke down, teachers discovered unforeseen advantages, social and educational, in mixed classes. When payment by results ended, children were grouped by age—with the bright ones pushed forward a year or two. These classes had a narrow spread of ages but a wide spread of attainment. Later as habits of classification became common in education, such schools as can, divide the year groups in 'A', 'B' or 'C'. This helped with the education of the bright 'A' child, and suited well with very formal methods of teaching, where everyone took the same lesson at the same time and speed. It also helped teachers to see some of the problems of the 'B' and 'C' groups separately, and created special techniques for handling backwardness.

Since 1944 it has usually been possible to withdraw the weakest children of all from normal schools.[1] New buildings and the reorganisation of schools make it possible for more and more head teachers to group children as 'A', 'B' and 'C', and the popular use of intelligence and attainment tests aids this. But criticisms are also being raised suggesting that it might be better to mix all such children together, and that modern teaching skills now make this possible.

This quick historical glance suggests that streaming emerged as a technique to reduce the special problems facing state education in the nineteen twenties and thirties. But as those problems alter, and as children, schools, teachers' skills and social values also changed, it developed from a temporary strategy into one of the settled institutions of our educational system.

---

[1] The 1944 Act defined eleven groups of children who must have special facilities: the blind, partially sighted, deaf, partially deaf, delicate, diabetic, epileptic, maladjusted, educationally sub-normal, physically handicapped and pupils suffering from speech defects. Children classified as mentally subnormal, were outside the provisions of the Education Acts. These groups are not included in the present discussion of streaming and non-streaming.

APPENDIX 3

LIST OF REFERENCES

BARR, F., 'Urban and Rural Differences in Attainment'. *Educational Research.* Vol. 1. No. 2. 1959.

BERNSTEIN, B., 'Social Class and Linguistic Development'. In HALSEY, A. H., FLOUD, J. E., and ANDERSON, C. A. (eds.), *Education, Economy and Society.* Illinois, Glencoe Free Press. 1961.

BURT, C., 'The Examination at Eleven Plus'. *British Journal of Educational Studies.* Vol. VII. No. 219. 1959.

BURT, C., 'Creativity and Intelligence' by JACKSON, P. W. and GETZELS, J. W.—A Review. *British Journal of Educational Psychology,* Vol. XXXII. Part 3. 1962.

COHEN, A. K., *Delinquent Boys: The Culture of the Gang.* London, Routledge & Kegan Paul. 1955.

DANIELS, J. C., 'Effects of Streaming in Primary Schools'. *British Journal of Educational Psychology.* Vol. XXXI. Parts 1 and 2. 1961.

DENT, H. C., *Secondary Education for All.* London, Routledge & Kegan Paul. 1949.

DOUGLAS, J. W. B. and BLOOMFIELD, J. M., *Children under Five.* London, Allen and Unwin. 1958.

DOUGLAS, J. W. B., *The Home and the School.* London, MacGibbon and Kee. 1964.

DOUGLAS, J. W. B. and ROWNTREE, G., *Maternity in Great Britain.* London, Oxford University Press. 1948.

DOUGLAS, J. W. B. and MULLIGAN, D. G., 'Emotional Adjustment and Educational Achievement'. *Proc. of Royal Society of Medicine.* Vol. 54. No. 10. 1961.

ELMGREN, J. K. G., *School and Psychology.* Stockholm, Nordiska bukhandeln. 1953.

FLOND, J. E., 'Social Class Factors in Educational Achievement' in HALSEY, A. H., FLOUD, J. E., and ANDERSON, C. A. (eds.) *Education, Economy and Society.* Illinois, Glencoe Free Press. 1961.

FITT, A. B., *Seasonal Influence on Growth, Function and Inheritance.*

List of References

HIMMELWEIT, H. T., HALSEY, A. H. and OPPENHEIM, A. N. 'The Views of Adolescents on Some Aspects of the Social Class Structure'. *British Journal of Sociology.* Vol. III. No. 2. 1952.

HASEN, T., 'Educational Structure and the Development of Ability' in HALSEY, A. H. (ed.), *Ability and Educational Opportunity.* Paris, O.E.C.D. 1961.

JACKSON, B., 'Teachers' Views on Primary School Streaming'. *Educational Research.* Vol. IV. No. 1. 1961.

JACKSON, P. W. and GETZELS, J. W. *Creativity and Intelligence.* London and New York, John Wiley. 1962.

KELSALL, R. K. 'Getting on at the Grammar'. *Times Educational Supplement,* Mar. 15th 1963.

LEE, H. D. P., *Plato's Republic* (trans.) Harmondsworth, Penguin Books. 1955.

LEES, J. P. and STEWART, A. H., 'Family or Sibship, Position and Scholastic Ability'. *Sociological Review.* Vol. 5. Nos. 1 and 2. 1957.

LOWNDES, G. A. N., *The Silent Social Revolution.* Oxford. 1937.

LYNN, R., 'Environmental Conditions affecting Intelligence'. *Educational Research.* Vol. 1. No. 3. 1959.

MILLER, T. W. G. *Values in the Comprehensive School.* Edinburgh, Oliver and Boyd. 1961.

ORME, J. E. 'Intelligence, Season of Birth and Climate Temperature'. *British Journal of Psychology.* Vol. 54, Part 3. 1963.

PAPE, G. V. 'Accident of Birth'. *Education,* Nov. 16th, 1956.

ROBERTS, FRASER, J. A. 'Intelligence and the Season of Conception'. *British Medical Journal.* Vol. 1. 1964.

RUDD, W. G. A. 'The Effects of Streaming—a Further Contribution'. *Educational Research.* Vol. II. No. 3. 1960.

SEMMENS, H. 'Rural Reorganisation'. *Journal of Education.* Vol. 90. No. 1064. 1958.

STEWART, M. *The Success of the First Born Child.* London, Workers' Educational Association. 1962.

SUTHERLAND, E. H., *Principles of Criminology.* Chicago, Lippincott. 1955.

SVENSSON, N. E. 'Ability Grouping and Scholastic Attainment'. *Educational Research.* Vol. V. No. 1. 1962.

TURNER, R. H. 'Modes of Social Ascent through Education' in HALSEY, A. H., FLOUD, J. E. and ANDERSON, C. A. (eds.), *Education, Economy and Society.* Illinois, Glencoe Free Press, 1961.

WILKINS, L. T. *Delinquent Generations.* London, H.M.S.O. 1961.

WILLIS, C. J. 'Social Implications of Streaming in Junior School'. *Educational Research.* Vol. V. No. 2. 1963.

YATES, A. and PIDGEON, D. A. 'The Effects of Streaming'. *Educational Research*. Vol. II. No. 1. 1959.

Board of Education. *Handbook of Suggestions for Teachers*. London, H.M.S.O. 1937.

Central Advisory Council for Education. *Half Our Future*. London. H.M.S.O. 1963.

Central Advisory Council for Education. *15 to 18*. London. H.M.S.O. 1959.

Consultative Committees. *The Education of the Adolescent*. London. H.M.S.O. 1926.

Ministry of Education. *The Nation's Schools*. Ministry of Education. Pamphlet No. 1. 1945.

Ministry of Education. *Primary Education*. London. H.M.S.O. 1959.

National Foundation for Educational Research. '*Procedures for the Allocation of Pupils in Secondary Education.*' London, N.F.E.R., 1963.

UNESCO Institute of Education, Hamburg. '*Educational Achievements of Thirteen-Year-Olds in Twelve Countries*', Hamburg, UNESCO, 1962.

West Riding Education Authority. '*Memorandum on Streaming*', 1962.

TEACHING IN UNSTREAMED SCHOOLS

I know of no adequate book to help the teacher of an unstreamed primary class, but I myself have learned a lot, in very different ways, from the following books and journals.

SYBIL MARSHALL. *An Experiment in Education*. Cambridge University Press. 1963.

BRIAN SIMON (ed.), *New Trends in English Education*. Lawrence & Wishart. 1957.

DORA PYM. *Free Writing*. University of London Press. 1956.

A. W. ROWE. *The Education of the Average Child*. Harrap. 1960.

L. G. W. SEALEY. *Creative Mathematics*. Blackwell. 1960.

EDWARD BLISHEN (ed.), *Changing Schools*. Council for Children's Welfare. 1959.

A. B. CLEGG (ed.) *The Excitement of Writing*. Chatto & Windus. 1964.

Forum. (PSW Educational Publications, 71 Clarendon Park Road, Leicester.)

Educational Research. (Newnes, for the National Foundation for Educational Research.)

The Use of English (Chatto & Windus.)

Where? (Advisory Centre for Education, 57 Russell Street, Cambridge.)

INDEX

155

Index